D0599545

The L. Ron Hubbard Series

BRIDGE PUBLICATIONS, INC.
5600 E. Olympic Blvd.
Commerce, California 90022 USA

ISBN 978-1-4031-9885-3

© 1995, 2012 L. Ron Hubbard Library. All Rights Reserved.

Any unauthorized copying, translation, duplication, importation or distribution, in whole or in part, by any means, including electronic copying, storage or transmission, is a violation of applicable laws.

Special acknowledgment is made to the L. Ron Hubbard Library for permission to reproduce photographs from his personal collection. Additional credits: pp. cover, 20 Keystone Press Agency/Hulton Archive; pp. 1, 7, 21, 31, 59, 73, 105, 117, back cover Norbi/Shutterstock.com; p. 24 Adam Fraise/Shutterstock.com; pp. 68/69 kk-artworks/Shutterstock.com; pp. 122/123 Adisa/Shutterstock.com.

Dianetics, Scientology, Freewinds, Golden Era Productions, Hubbard, L. Ron Hubbard, LRH, Clearsound, Clearsound Logo, Saint Hill, Sea Org Symbol, L. Ron Hubbard Signature and *Ron Signature* are trademarks and service marks owned by Religious Technology Center and are used with its permission.

Scientologist is a collective membership mark designating members of the affiliated churches and missions of Scientology.

The Way to Happiness and *Mission Earth* (words and fist & globe) are trademarks owned by L. Ron Hubbard Library and are used with permission. *Battlefield Earth* is a trademark owned by Author Services, Inc., and is used with permission.

Bridge Publications, Inc. is a registered trademark and service mark in California and it is owned by Bridge Publications, Inc.

NEW ERA is a trademark and service mark owned by New Era Publications International ApS and is registered in Denmark, among other countries.

Printed in the United States of America

The L. Ron Hubbard Series: Music Maker—English

The L. Ron Hubbard Series

MUSIC MAKER
COMPOSER
& PERFORMER

PUBLICATIONS, INC. ®

CONTENTS

An Introduction to
L. Ron Hubbard

OW AND WHY THE FOUNDER OF DIANETICS AND Scientology came to involve himself so deeply in music may seem difficult to grasp, remarked a critic some years ago. "Nonetheless, he has put together a highly energized big band. And in doing so, has solved a problem the likes of which Buddy Rich and even Woody Herman failed to do. That is, focus the energy of a combo in a big band, a feat which is like harnessing the atom."

In fact, L. Ron Hubbard harnessed far more through his lifelong devotion to music. But the how and why of it is not at all difficult to fathom—not when one considers his larger devotion to the arts as an award-winning photographer, a celebrated screenwriter, an accomplished poet and among the most acclaimed and widely read novelists of this or any age. Then, too, and particularly as the Founder of Scientology, music became that universal language with which he worked "to rejoice the greatest souls."

Welcome to the story of L. Ron Hubbard, Music Maker, and yet another side of a man who legitimately lived twenty lives in the space of one—in this case as a musical director, arranger, performer and composer. And if he never counted himself a professional musician in the strictest sense, this is nonetheless a story of cutting-edge innovation across a dozen forms and musical styles.

To cite but a few of the high notes: among the first to tap the potential of computerized music, his incorporation of natural sounds into the actual fabric of songs was at least a decade ahead of its time, while his mid-1970s essays on musical structure and instrumentation continue to influence professionals far and wide. He was further the first to compose literary soundtracks—specifically to his internationally bestselling novels *Battlefield Earth* and *Mission Earth*—then proceeded to redefine our entire conception of religious music with his Scientology musical statement, *The Road to Freedom.* Then there is all he brought to music through his overall analysis

An informal New Year's Eve performance,
Washington, DC, 1957

"A true professional may do things pretty easily from all appearances, but he is actually taking care with each little bit that it is just right."

—*L. Ron Hubbard*

Right
Tacoma, Washington, circa 1923: on the eve of adventures wherein he would hear music altogether alien to Western ears

Far right
Outside Peking, China, 1928: through extended Asian travels, Ron studied numerous musical forms unique to the Orient

of the medium—how music best conveys emotion, how it excites, how it lulls and how, ultimately, as he wrote: "You can do anything you want to with it to make it communicate the intended message."

There is more, including his dissection of musical expression back to the very dawn of human existence, and his analysis of popular trends still unfolding to this day. But lest we move ahead of our story, let us simply say here lies a trail of musical discovery spanning many forms, many cultures and many decades. Indeed, L. Ron Hubbard's musical journey very nearly parallels his greater life's journey and through the course of it, he analyzed more than a dozen musical styles—from country western to Far Eastern, from high Baroque to low Amazonian, from classical to tribal. In consequence, and this too is a keynote of our story, he drew upon every heritage encountered to develop a truly international musical vocabulary.

He was also admirably proficient on at least as many instruments—from his Montana banjo to a Guamanian billibutugun (fashioned from a cocoanut and played on the abdomen), from harmonicas and ukuleles to the then singularly most advanced electronic synthesizers. Just for good measure, there was his famously expressive baritone with which he entertained listeners in a radio slot that launched Arthur Godfrey, and his wonderfully perceptive ear with which he dissected sound behavior to inspire what has been described as the finest recording facility in the world.

Like every art form, Ron noted, music is designed to tell a story, and the story of his own musical legacy is a vast one. That it properly begins in the American West of his youth is to be expected; after all, his music was a lifelong pursuit. But that his legacy encompasses not merely composition, performance or arranging, but the entirety of this evocative universal language—that is uniquely L. Ron Hubbard. ∎

CHAPTER ONE

A Musical HERITAGE

A Musical
Heritage

To begin with, L. Ron Hubbard's musical heritage came with the landscape of his youth. Among other early memories, he would tell of his great-grandfather sawing away on a country fiddle through warm Oklahoma afternoons. With the Hubbard family's move to Montana in 1913, the primary strains remained typically Western:

indigenous campfire ballads, cowboy bands and the lilting reels of country hoedowns. In a later essay on the subject, he would rightly point out that such strains were soon to be lost in a blander Hollywood interpretation, e.g., Roy Rogers and Gene Autry. But the original, as he would long maintain, had been absolutely compelling—a spontaneous and gregarious music that will always "linger in people's memories." Also of notable influence through his youth were the actual roots of the country sound, including surviving melodies brought in by Irish railroad workers

and the so-called forty-niner laments of mining camp life and dying cowboys. Less an influence, but still worth noting, was the classical piano, studied under an elderly relative. Otherwise he was self-taught on the saxophone, banjo and mouth organ.

His first public performance appears to have been an impromptu affair in Great Falls, Montana, where, as he colorfully noted in a 1928 diary: "Dunc and I bought mouth organs and played on the street while the big boy Bert of Wyoming played a tin drum and Sapp passed around the hat." The mouth organ, incidentally,

Left
Ron's
Great-grandfather
Waterbury with
the country fiddle
for which he was
regionally famed

Left Helena, Montana: Ron (center) and schoolmates with whom he formed an impromptu band

HARMONICA: "You can't go lugging around a piano," Ron remarked, "not when you led as ambulant and as traveled a life as me." His solution was the harmonica, or mouth organ, as he generally referred to it. From the late 1920s forward, he was rarely without one and actually kept several, in varying keys, in a footlocker beneath his bed. His ability with the instrument was said to have been legendary, and even decades later fellow musicians would tell of the day he performed an "absolutely smokin' blues version" of "Oh, Susanna" on a four-note harmonica picked up at a penny arcade.

would long remain a favored instrument, mainly because of its convenience. He was eventually to collect several dozen in varying sizes and keys and would always carry them during his far-flung travels.

Those famous travels, most notable as the first leg of discovery to Dianetics and Scientology, commenced in 1927 with his father's posting at the United States Naval Station on the island of Guam. Following by way of China and Japan, the sixteen-year-old Ron encountered what was to be the first of many remote musical traditions—in this case that curious Guamanian blend of native Chamorro, Spanish and what passed for swing in dance halls catering to Americans. Of particular note was the billibutugun which he detailed

Top
Among other musical curiosities encountered through his South Pacific voyages was the billibutugun (carried by Chamorro native on left)

Bottom
The billibutugun, comprised of a wooden stick, baling wire and a cocoanut shell, is played against the abdomen. Hence, Ron's comment "the larger the stomach, the better the tone."

BANJO: Inherited from his maternal grandfather and namesake, Lafayette "Lafe" Waterbury, the five-string banjo was very much a part of Ron's musical heritage. Used by Lafe in minstrel shows through the late 1800s, banjos of this type were also part and parcel of the distinctive Western sound of Ron's youth. As he later pointed out, it was essentially an imported sound, derived from balladeers aboard Mississippi steamboats. It was entirely fitting, then, that he, too, used Lafe's five-string banjo while a balladeer on radio WOL, Washington, DC.

Ron's turn-of-the-century five-string banjo was manufactured by a Birmingham, England, company

5 String Banjo about 1880 – Property of Lafe Waterbury LRH's Grandfather. Used by him in Minstrel Shows. Used by LRH while Balladeer Stn WOL, DC. 1930

in another diary entry as "It is about seven feet long and has a piece of baling wire strung across it. They hold the wire taut by the spring of the stick and place the cocoanut, which is nailed to the center of the stick, on their stomachs. It is said that the larger the stomach, the better the tone."

Following a brief return to Helena, Montana—where he picked up his sax to play in a basement band—Ron again set out across the South Pacific to a then still-mysterious Asia. There, he studied unique instrumentation that would surface in several later compositions, including the tribal war drums of Mongolian horsemen, the gamelan gongs of the Javanese temple orchestras, the Japanese koto, the Indian sitar and the Chinese zither. A later

Above
Washington, DC, circa 1930: while attending George Washington University (left), Ron performed ballads of his own composition on local radio WOL

note further references a blue silk bag of "twenty or thirty various kinds of instruments" and adds, "I can play anything on a carpenter's saw." But more to the point, it was through the course of these Asian travels that he first explored the possibility of what he described as the "unpositive note" or that strangely apologetic quality so characteristic of the Asian music. That is, as he later explained, the traditionally low-caste Asian musician could not arrogantly strike a note. Thus notes are periodically approached from below and the musician slides up to it slowly, i.e., "One apologetically slides up to it or down to it."

On his return to the United States in 1929, and while launching his literary career as a student at George Washington University, Ron made his first fully professional

"...it was through the course of these Asian travels that he first explored the possibility of what he described as the 'unpositive note.'"

UKULELE: Purchased in Hawaii in 1927, the four-string ukulele was to serve L. Ron Hubbard through the next four decades. Most memorably, this was the instrument with which he entertained Washington, DC, radio listeners in a slot that would later launch Arthur Godfrey. It also cheered fellow seamen aboard ships en route to China and served him in jam sessions on the island of Guam. How the normally fragile instrument survived those decades, not to mention the quarter of a million miles of travel, is something of a mystery. In either case, his distinctive "Pineapple" Uke was further remembered by students at the Saint Hill Hubbard College, where Ron used it for impromptu concerts through the mid-1960s.

This five-string timple was manufactured in Santa Cruz de Tenerife, Canary Islands

appearance as radio WOL's balladeer. Although no recordings exist, he was said to have entertained listeners with a superbly fine baritone and a Hawaiian ukulele. Through the remainder of the 1930s, he continued performing on a casual basis, but clearly never lost his professional edge, as evidenced by his next radio slot.

To abbreviate a long and adventurous story: The summer of 1940 found L. Ron Hubbard heading a nautical expedition from his Port Orchard, Washington, home through the British Columbian passage to the Alaskan Panhandle. The voyage, conducted on behalf of the United States Navy's Hydrographic Office and aimed at charting treacherous inland waterways, had also taken him deep into Native American habitats for ethnological

The Martin ten-string, otherwise known as an "American Tiple." Designed by C. F. Martin & Company in the early 1920s, the tiple is an instrument common to Latin America (*tiple* from Spanish for "treble" or "soprano"). The Martin Tiple features ten steel strings in four "courses," tuned like a ukulele. Received as a gift in the early 1980s, Ron's Martin ten-string is arguably the finest of all American Tiples and was manufactured at the Martin Factory in Nazareth, Pennsylvania.

research. Yet landing at the Alaskan port of Ketchikan, and owing to his renown as both author and mariner, he received another invitation to the airwaves.

The station was the "Voice of Alaska," radio KGBU, headed and hosted by local personality Jimmy Britton. The territory's only chain broadcast facility, radio KGBU catered to listeners all along the lower Alaskan coast and thus offered several shows for yachtsmen and fisherfolk. Ron's slot, entitled "Mail Buoy," was typical. Listeners with questions on any and all nautical matters were invited to address their queries to master mariner L. Ron Hubbard, who would promptly air his replies. But in addition to his very sound advice on the trimming of sails or onboard fire prevention, he also entertained.

Ron's Venezuelan cuatro, manufactured in the northern state of Carabobo

Top
Transmission tower, radio KGBU Ketchikan, the "Voice of Alaska"

Above
The KGBU in-house orchestra

Right
In the KGBU broadcast booth where Ron performed ballads for Alaskan listeners up and down the Panhandle

Again, no recordings were made. Written transcripts, however, offer not only dialogue, but the lyrics of ballads he wrote and performed. Typical is his hauntingly beautiful "The Alaska Chief," inspired by the loss of a cannery fleet vessel off the rocky Dover shore, and apparently performed with either ukulele or guitar:

> *The next to go was A. M. Accue*
> *Fighting as a seaman can*
> *He swam an hour in the icy sea*
> *And drowned with the shore in scan*
>
> *He must have known that the bitter fight*
> *Was against the ebbing tide*
> *He surely knew but he never stopped*
> *But swimming, sank and died*

For the next several years thereafter, Ron appears precisely as portrayed by acclaimed

Ron played this classical six-string guitar in the early 1960s

editor and colleague John W. Campbell, Jr.: an immensely talented, if occasional, musician: "He's fully as good as Bing Crosby or Lawrence Tibbett—with an effect sort of halfway between those two." In an especially evocative note, Campbell describes an L. Ron Hubbard performance in these terms: "He has a low, magnificently mellow baritone voice, and he 'puts over' a song so powerfully that, when he's finished, there's a very sharply noticeable pause of dead silence before anyone speaks or shifts to make small noises in the semidark." As a further note on repertoire, Campbell correctly spoke of songs Ron had picked up "here, there and everywhere," including a prewar Asiatic Fleet's "The Armored Cruiser Squadron" and

"He has a low, magnificently mellow baritone voice, and he 'puts over' a song so powerfully that, when he's finished, there's a very sharply noticeable pause of dead silence before anyone speaks or shifts to make small noises in the semidark."

Ron's four-string tenor guitar

"Fifteen Men on a Dead Man's Chest," which, as the editor explained, may have lost something through association with the film *Treasure Island,* but became altogether "spine-chilling and blood-curdling when Ron sings it by firelight."

Also from these years come accounts of Ron's versatility on the keyboard, which he seems to have picked up between that series of lessons in Helena and ballroom pianos in naval station dance halls. Then there was the night he led a rhumba line on voodoo drums he had mastered through the course of Caribbean expeditions. "The amount of rhythm one can extract from a drum with the hands is remarkable," he noted, and told of a "throb and moan and wail and roll and thunder and whisper like a parade of ghosts."

Yet regardless of how seemingly peripheral were his musical pursuits through these years, the outcome was by no means peripheral. In fact, it was just such a pursuit that would finally lead him to the central revelation of all musical creativity—including that riveting aesthetic power John Campbell had sensed when he wrote of the "very sharply noticeable pause of dead silence before anyone speaks or shifts to make small noises in the semidark." ∎

CHAPTER TWO

The
ART OF MUSIC

The
Art of Music

JUST AS IT IS IMPOSSIBLE TO APPRECIATE THE WHOLE OF L. Ron Hubbard's life without his music, so too, one cannot appreciate his music without taking into account what he gave artistic endeavor as a whole.

The subject had long intrigued him; for until one could offer a workable definition of art, he had written, the world was not likely to become more conscious of it. And without art, as he elsewhere added, a society's honor and glory is lost.

So between all else that occupied him in the name of Dianetics and Scientology, L. Ron Hubbard examined musical form and its emotional response as part of his larger study of aesthetics. At the heart of this examination lay a very special view of Man as an intrinsically spiritual being who was himself quite close to all that is embodied in the words *beautiful* and *aesthetics*. And, in fact, he explained, when one speaks of utilizing Dianetics and Scientology toward the rehabilitation of artistic ability, one is speaking of rehabilitating that which is closest to our spiritual heart. But the problem of providing a workable definition of art remained, and partially to that end, L. Ron Hubbard

continued his examination of what is probably the most ubiquitous of all artistic forms—music.

His preferred instrument for such research was the electronic organ. The first, a Baldwin 10 Electronic Organ, served him in Wichita, Kansas, where, between the spring of 1951 and the winter of 1952, he lectured at the local Dianetics Foundation. With his founding of Scientology and its worldwide growth through the remainder of the decade came Ron's move to Saint Hill Manor in East Grinstead, Sussex. There, beside an apartment piano, stood a Wurlitzer and much prized Mellotron electric keyboard instrument—forerunner of the synthesizer and capable of replicating the human voice. In a closing sequence of a Scientology promotional film entitled *An Afternoon at Saint Hill,* he is seen at the instrument for a rendition of "When the Saints Go Marching In." His own compositions from the era have been described as faintly medieval

Wurlitzer and Mellotron at Saint Hill Manor, England

and hauntingly beautiful. But the main end to what he modestly termed this incidental study was an understanding of music in general and art as a whole.

His now famous conclusions are contained in a revelatory text entitled *ART*. The most broadly influential philosophic explanation of the creative process, *ART* has inspired artists of a dozen fields, including writing, painting, filmmaking, acting, dance and, of course, music. Intrinsic to the work is his much quoted definition of art as "a word which summarizes THE QUALITY OF COMMUNICATION." It is within that framework, then, that he proceeded to codify the subject in its entirety.

By way of example, consider his analysis of rhythm. "There are six distinct types of rhythm in music," begins his examination of the matter as contained in *ART*. He then continues with his definitive analysis of those rhythmical types, including:

"REGULAR: Meaning the evenly accented (stressed) beat.

"SYNCOPATED: The placing of upbeats along with downbeats at regular or irregular intervals.

"STOPPED: In a stopped rhythm there are regular distinct halts to the flow of melody, but all the beats are there, they are simply regularly halted for an interval.

"ACCENTED: Where one or more beats in a measure received a stronger stress (beat) or accent.

"OMITTED BEAT: The regular omission of one or more beats in measures.

"ADDED BEAT: Additional strong or, generally, weak beats are added to the rhythm in a consistent or inconsistent manner."

His point—and he was first to recognize such a delineation—any and all rhythms are made up of those six basic forms, singularly or in combination, and it is the skillful employment of these rhythms that establishes audience rapport and thus communication. In the same essay he further delineates the use of rhythm to either lull, soothe or excite, and the role of rhythm in prose, poetry and even the visual arts. For in the final analysis, he very acutely observed, "Rhythm and its expression is the basic key to all art forms."

Also pertinently addressed through the pages of *ART* are the fundamentals of presentation, of which he declared: "Artistic presentation always succeeds to the degree that it is done *well*. How *easily* it is done is entirely secondary." Thus, "A true professional may do things pretty easily

Types of Rhythm

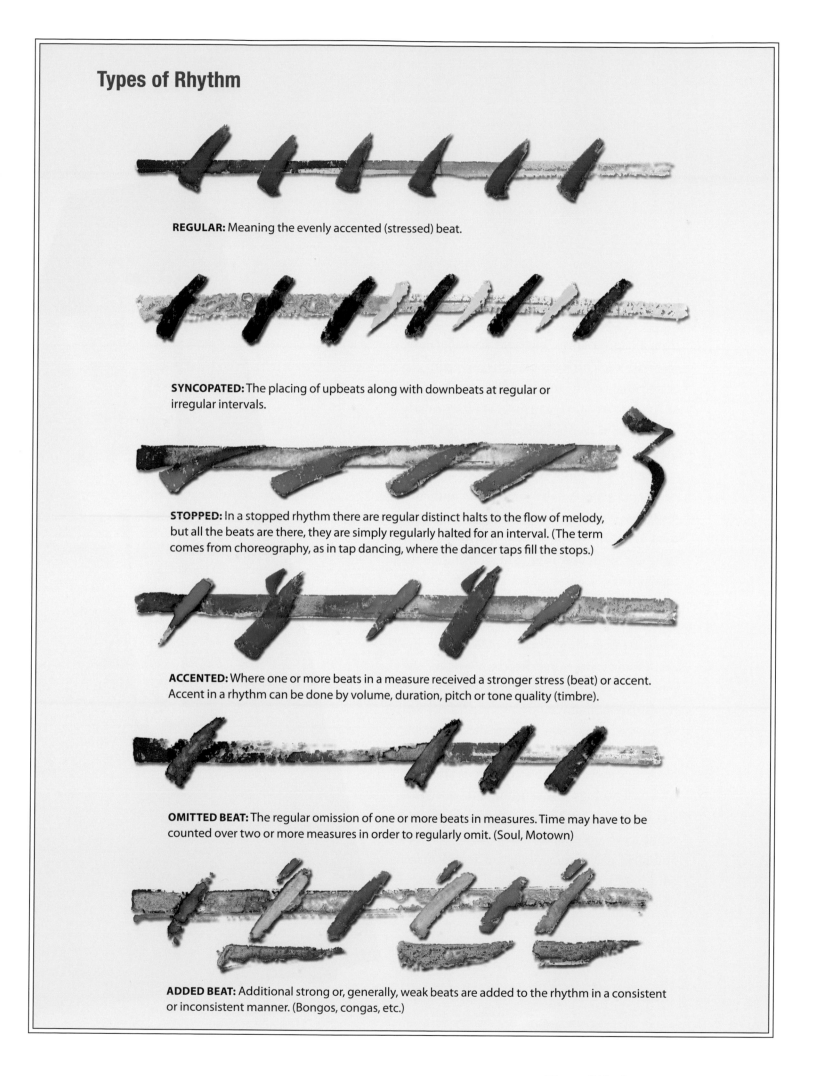

REGULAR: Meaning the evenly accented (stressed) beat.

SYNCOPATED: The placing of upbeats along with downbeats at regular or irregular intervals.

STOPPED: In a stopped rhythm there are regular distinct halts to the flow of melody, but all the beats are there, they are simply regularly halted for an interval. (The term comes from choreography, as in tap dancing, where the dancer taps fill the stops.)

ACCENTED: Where one or more beats in a measure received a stronger stress (beat) or accent. Accent in a rhythm can be done by volume, duration, pitch or tone quality (timbre).

OMITTED BEAT: The regular omission of one or more beats in measures. Time may have to be counted over two or more measures in order to regularly omit. (Soul, Motown)

ADDED BEAT: Additional strong or, generally, weak beats are added to the rhythm in a consistent or inconsistent manner. (Bongos, congas, etc.)

from all appearances, but he is actually taking care with each little bit that it is just right." To exactly that end, he further addressed the more or less lost art of stage manners (a particularly interesting matter in light of shock rock). But the fact is, and regardless of how seemingly contemptuous is the snide rock performer, "a degree of affinity with or for the audience must be physically expressed." For in the final analysis, the purpose of performance is basically communication and, drawing from a fundamental Scientology tenet, communication is impossible in the absence of affinity.

There is more, including his analysis of musical integration wherein melody matches rhythm and tonality matches the mood, and still more again on eliciting audience contribution in terms of motion and emotion. On a personal note, we are told Ron's own performances, however impromptu, were models of all he advised. In black tie at a concert grand to entertain attendees of a Scientology convention, the word was "polished elegance." Every gesture positive and refined, every note and vocal inflection flawless and, all in all, the embodiment of a music maker whose work indeed "summarizes the quality of communication." ■

RHYTHM: Any kind of movement characterized by the regular recurrence of strong and weak elements. Rhythm denotes the regular patterned flow, the ebb and rise of sounds and movement in speech, music, writing, dance and in other physical activities.

> *"When a work of painting, music or other form attains two-way communication, it is truly art."*
> —*L. Ron Hubbard*

A Collection of Rare Musical Instruments

Throughout his life, L. Ron Hubbard sought out and obtained instruments from virtually every corner of the world. His collection is as wide and varied as the cultures he researched. Below is a brief description of just some of the more unusual instruments contained in Ron's collection.

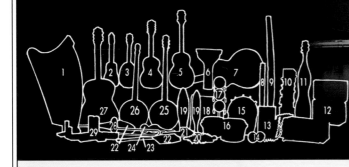

1. Gaelic harp acquired in Ireland, 1956
2. Five-string timple
3. "Pineapple" Uke
4. Martin ten-string "Tiple"
5. Venezuelan baritone cuatro
6. Syrian drum
7. Four-string tenor guitar
8. African wind instrument
9. Australian didgeridoo
10. Himalayan stringed instrument, played with a bow, common to Afghanistan and Nepal
11. Appalachian cherry-wood dulcimer
12. African split wooden drums (Gatos)
13. African shaker instruments
14. Maracas
15. Native African drums
16. Bongos

17. "Spin drums" spun back and forth, causing the strikers at the end of strings to beat on the small drums
18. African square drum
19. Hollow wooden sounders
20. Castanets acquired in Spain, 1953
21. Aborigine rhythm sticks
22. African thumb pianos
23. Bamboo flute
24. Maracas
25. Turn-of-the-century five-string banjo
26. 1880 five-string banjo
27. Classical six-string guitar
28. English-crafted trombone
29. Hohner harmonicas

The Apollo Stars performing aboard an "Apollo" float: Cádiz, Spain, 1974

CHAPTER THREE

MUSICAL DIRECTOR

Musical Director

GIVEN HIS CONTINUED DEVOTION TO THE DEVELOPMENT and expansion of Scientology, it was not until late 1973 that Ron was again able to devote himself to music in any concerted manner. The setting was his research vessel, *Apollo,* then at sea in the Mediterranean and Atlantic, and from where he informed a British arranger/composer:

"It occurred to me that as we had some musicians on board scattered amongst the crew, we should form an organization known as the Apollo Troupe." The referenced crew were members of Scientology's Sea Organization, founded in 1967 to support Ron's research and otherwise forward the growth of Scientology. In addition to all other benefits to be had from the formation of a shipboard troupe was Ron's abiding concern the *Apollo* supply some form of exchange with those ports regularly providing dockage and hospitality. Consequently, and given the nautical tradition of shipboard bands, he logically posed the question: Why not organize a musical troupe in the name of port-side goodwill and cultural exchange?

It began in earnest with a hastily prepared performance at a winter festival on the Portuguese island of Madeira. If the audience was not particularly sophisticated—under a rightist regime much popular music had not made its way to Portugal—Madeira residents were nonetheless discerning, with a rich musical heritage of dances and ballads. Although three of the original seventeen performers could claim some professional experience, the remainder were strictly amateur—garage-band musicians, as it was said, and only remotely capable of a cohesive performance. Still, under Ron's tutelage—and he would initially drill them note by note—the Madeira debut in a municipal band shell proved

As Musical Director of the regionally famed Apollo Troupe, 1974

Above
Shipboard with his Apollo Troupe, for whom he regularly composed, arranged and choreographed performances

an unqualified success and the first of the Apollo Troupe, the Apollo Stars, was born.

At the outset, the repertoire was most accurately described as popular jazz, i.e., jazz versions of Gershwin standards and the like. In addition to drums, bass and guitars, instrumentation soon included brass, keyboards and flute. That not all were especially proficient was only of slight concern, for in absolute application was the LRH dictum: an artist should drill with his equipment until he feels confident with it.

A host of drills were eventually prescribed in the name of confidence and technical expertise. Some, for the development of those basic skills possessed by any competent musician, were traditional—or variations on traditional drills. For example, recalled the drummer, "He would relentlessly drill us with metronomes, which, of course, is standard fare. But rather than drilling only individually, he would utilize the metronome to instill rhythmical skills for the group as a whole." By way of illustration, musicians told of tapping their feet to the steady beat of an electronic metronome. The group would continue to tap out the beat while the volume of the metronome was turned down until it was inaudible. After sixty to one hundred seconds, the volume would be turned back up again, "and the whole group was expected to be tapping out the beat, exactly in time to the electronic device—not faster or slower, but dead on!"

The fundamental point: "Ron was relentlessly driving home the basics to us as a team, because without the basics you have no art."

The statement was crucial both to the success of the musicians as a troupe and as artists individually. For drawn from his *ART* was an absolutely key datum delineating just how good the musician, or any artist for that matter, must be:

"If you look at or listen to any work of art, there is only one thing the casual audience responds to en masse. And if this has it, then you too will see it as a work of art. If it doesn't have it, you won't.

"So what is *it?*

"TECHNICAL EXPERTISE ITSELF ADEQUATE TO PRODUCE AN EMOTIONAL IMPACT."

Left L. Ron Hubbard's yacht *Apollo,* from whence came his sweeping analyses of musical forms, styles, elements and trends

"Living itself can be an art."—LRH

A perfectly musical seafaring moment aboard the schooner, *Doris Hamlin*, en route to the southern latitudes

Ron's 1932 nautical expedition to Caribbean pirate haunts

The Sea Chanteys

With L. Ron Hubbard's move to his research vessel *Apollo* in the late 1960s, and the formation of the Sea Organization to both assist that research and forward Scientology, a spontaneous musical tradition sprang up as part of shipboard culture. Appropriately, ship's officers fondly recall Ron singing sea chanteys from memory, usually self-accompanied with ukulele.

The chantey had long been an LRH favorite. As early as 1932, he had entertained crews of vessels with such songs and was factually somewhat of an expert on piratical lore—the leader of a nautical expedition to explore Caribbean pirate haunts and author of the 1930s Hollywood film, *The Secret of Treasure Island*. The point being: he brought that fabulous world of sea dogs to life with an authority few balladeers could manage and so kept a nautical tradition of music alive for the Sea Organization crew. ■

In direct application came a dozen more LRH drills—all wholly original. For instance, having previously noted that music alone might soothe, lull or excite to any of the fifty-nine emotions delineated by the Scientology Emotional Tone Scale, he called upon his musicians to literally practice eliciting that full range of emotion with only instrumentation. Similarly, he instructed musicians to compose melodies that regardless of beat or instrumentation would elicit such emotions as apathy, enthusiasm or serenity. Finally, and in keeping with his emphasis on music as an actual means of communication, he encouraged performers to practice eliciting whole scenarios with only musical riffs—as in the drummer who found himself developing riffs to convey such scenarios as a drunken disco dancer or a haughty cat. "Which at first seemed nearly impossible," he explained, "but little by little I was able to make those drums describe exactly that haughty cat or drunk dancer."

The implicit point, as Ron explained: "Music isn't mechanics. It's sound and emotional message, and you can do anything you want to with it."

Additionally borne out in these first few weeks was the genuinely impressive scope of Ron's own expertise. Meeting with musicians at, say, nine-thirty in the evening, he might offer the melodic basis of a new composition, often little more than a whistled tune. Then working out lyrics, drum fills and bass, he would lead his troupe through a rough take or two. What with rehearsal and polish, the song was then ready for a routinely well-received performance—all within twenty-four hours. On yet another occasion, this time working through a single night, Ron actually developed an entirely new repertoire comprising a full two-hour performance. Nor was he limited to any one style, but could just as quickly compose in country western, Oriental and Middle Eastern. He was also to serve as musical director, instructor, composer, arranger, recordist and mixer...until, in fact, there was finally no aspect of the *Apollo* sound that did not bear his imprint.

Concurrently, and wholly independently, the early weeks of 1974 saw the start of what Ron described as his analysis of modern musical trends. Again, his tools were derived from basic Scientology principles relating to logic and the evaluation of data. In a simple description of the process, he told of digesting recordings of popular groups—everything from acid rock to rockabilly—with an eye to "get something like a reach forward beyond the current trend." In fact, it proved an exhaustive task that would ultimately involve

> *"Studying the more popular groups, listening to their 'singing,' listening to their arrangements, instrumentation and drum shifts of emphasis to sticks and by other signs, it became fairly visible, at least to me, that the sophisticated world was rolling back into the past and reaching for its tribal roots."*
>
> —L. Ron Hubbard

an analysis of several thousand recordings from what amounted to a global catalog of music—everything from high classical and country western, to the Hispanic and Middle Eastern strains that dictated tastes in local ports of call. His conclusion—particularly interesting, given the increasingly complex orchestration of the mid-1970s—proved absolutely correct. To put it bluntly, he wrote, "I analyzed it this way: that music is going more and more primitive."

He then proceeded with an explanation that, in light of later punk and rap trends, is altogether inarguable:

"Studying the more popular groups, listening to their 'singing,' listening to their arrangements, instrumentation and drum shifts of emphasis to sticks and by other signs, it became fairly visible, at least to me, that the sophisticated world was rolling back into the past and reaching for its tribal roots. The savage breast was stirred by rhythms mostly because they had very little in the way of instruments. But it seems the savage breast is with us again and is stirred by derivations from primitive sound. At least this is the way I looked at it."

The result he dubbed Star Sound and described it exactly in terms of that primitive theme reaching from "the future back to the cave" and thus rekindling what amounted to a tribal spirit of togetherness. "The world areas from which Star Sound is taken," he noted, "are (a) African, (b) West Indian, (c) South American, (d) Central American, (e) North American Native, (f) Mexican, (g) any cave or jungle period." While particularly in light of local Iberian tastes: "To the Star Sound has been added as well the folk or basic themes of Spain, Portugal and Europe, developing it so that it rekindles the tribal or community life." In that regard, Star Sound was not so much a musical form as a style of performance—gregarious, heavily syncopated, with strong reliance on percussion. Those who would see parallels to the subsequent popularization of the African sound through the likes of Paul Simon are correct. But it must be remembered that Star Sound was heard a full fifteen years before the general acceptance of such world music stars as Spain's Gipsy Kings or South Africa's Ladysmith Black Mambazo.

The net effect of this Star Sound was galvanizing. In the Portuguese town of Setúbal, for example, response to Star Sound proved so dramatic a normally staid crowd actually rushed the stage in a literal gesture of togetherness. (That the stage collapsed beneath their collective weight dampened no one's enthusiasm.)

Above right
"An audience in rapport PARTICIPATES in small or large ways with the performer or the artist or work of art, often by vocal or body motion."—LRH

Elsewhere, response was equally dramatic. A charity benefit for a Tenerife orphanage inspired yet another unbridled rush to a stage, while a performance before several thousand Funchal residents sparked a veritable riot. As a matter of fact, virtually every Apollo Stars performance ignited what amounted to a riot of enthusiasm; hence, the increasing requests for Apollo Stars performances—as many as four or five separate venues a week—increasing requests for recordings (the band was to enjoy fairly regular airplay on regional stations) and increasing concerns on the part of local authorities over crowd control. It was also at this point that *Apollo* musicians regularly found themselves besieged for autographs, mobbed for photographs and otherwise living up to their name.

With the Stars thus firmly established as the nucleus, the formation of several specialized groups commenced. In keeping with local tastes, these groups included a flamenco ensemble, replete with dancers, a Middle Eastern inspired vocalist and the contemporary Marineros offering then popular Progressiva—far-out pop. In no way,

however, was the creative scope of this period limited to local influences. Case in point was the formation of the Rangers, offering what Ron described as authentic country western, "per about 1870 tone quality." To achieve that sound, performers employed the "sharply Ozarked" mandolin, harsh fiddle and beats suggesting horse gaits: "walk, trot, canter, run and also single-foot, dance and park walk." Likewise drawing from his very personal musical vocabulary, Ron saw to the formation of the Troubadours, offering a distinctly Oriental sound—or, more accurately, Oriental

Left
That Ron frequently provided publicity shots of Apollo Star performances—incognito, from the press box, no less—is only too appropriate. For he was, after all, a world-class photographer quite in addition to Music Maker.

Below
Star Sound about to erupt in Lisbon, Portugal, 1974

*"One has to accept the fact that music itself
can communicate. It also can influence."*

—L. Ron Hubbard

*Right
The Power of
Source,* the
album critics
described in
these terms:
"L. Ron Hubbard
has put together
a highly
energized big
band. And
in doing so,
has solved a
problem the
likes of which
Buddy Rich and
even Woody
Herman failed
to do. That is,
focus the energy
of a combo in a
big band, a feat
which is like
harnessing the
atom."

music as it would have naturally evolved if not constrained by primitive instrumentation and caste restrictions. (In preparation, the Troubadours were required to not only familiarize themselves with various Asian cultures, but also replicate traditional Asian melodies.)

Also intrinsic to the Troupe's success was their employment of key LRH discoveries relating to performer-audience rapport. Most simply described as "keeping the audience with it," Ron defined that rapport in terms of "relationship, especially, one of mutual trust or affinity." Thus, "An audience in rapport is different than an audience of spectators. An audience in rapport PARTICIPATES in small or large ways with the performer or the artist or work of art, often by vocal or body motion."

Key to the attainment of rapport was, of course, Ron's discoveries pertaining to rhythm. For it was the rhythm, and particularly predictable rhythm, that most immediately invited audience participation. By way of illustration, yet another member of the Troupe tells of Ron developing a predictable rhythm for

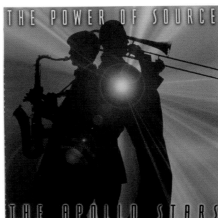

a given piece, and then actually choreographing band members' movements to further invite audience participation. The result was described as an entire hall in rhythmical rapport "so that all of us became part of the performance: musicians, audience, even the security forces and stagehands."

Utilizing this same principle, Ron addressed audience response to dance—which typically led him to an entire study of choreography as yet another medium by which one might successfully invite "clapping, stamping, yelling, even dancing."

Again, the net effect proved galvanizing—particularly when musicians were joined with Ron's choreographed and costumed dancers. For suddenly, and very dramatically, *Apollo* performers were presenting not only concerts, but whole theatrical displays, as in "The Dancing Tiger of Bali," a musical rendition of a Balinese folk myth. No less dramatic were the Star Dancers in highly evocative "Space-Primitive" garb with futuristic silver lamé suits and decorative bones for an LRH piece of the same name.

Then there was Ron's "Rain Dance."

"There is actually an amusing story connected with that Rain Dance," recalled another, and went on to explain how Ron had been working quite intently on choreography. "There had been his 'African Dance,' inspired by earlier research in Rhodesia, a uniquely primitive 'Amazon Dance' and finally 'The Rain Dance,' drawn from actual Blackfeet dances Ron had witnessed as a youth." Essentially a dance that said, *bring on rain,* "The first time we performed that dance it happened to take place during a period of weeks of dry, insufferable heat. The

dance was not only a hit with the locals, all of whom joined in, but coincidentally or not, it also rained later that day!"

With the *Apollo*'s passage to the Caribbean came Ron's elaborately performed calypso- and reggae-inspired dance and music, also well in advance of later international trends.

"One has to accept the fact that music itself can communicate," Ron wrote, and, in that regard, "it also can influence." How pervasive was that influence is difficult to gauge. Certainly his *Apollo* musicians earned much in terms of local appeal: Ron's tribute to the Spanish port of

Below
The Apollo Stars in concert at a Portuguese military base in Setúbal

Cádiz very literally stole the show at that city's annual *Gran Baile de Gala,* while his musicians were routinely mobbed at all other regular ports of call. Then, too, when a new Sea Organization vessel, *Freewinds,* appeared at Curaçao some twelve years after the last *Apollo* performance, local residents approached ship's officers to ask, "Have you come back to play for us?"

Yet considering all else Ron had to say about music through this period—his delineation of rhythm, his analysis of musical presentation and his uncanny ability to anticipate trends years in advance of the fact—his influence clearly extended much further. ■

In the trailing summer of 1931, with the wind as his compass and a toothbrush for baggage, Ron set out on a barnstorming tour of the American Midwest. His craft was an Arrow Sport biplane and airstrips were whatever field would accommodate a landing. Accordingly, he tells of touching down one evening in a cow pasture and coming upon an authentic square dance. Among other notable observations: the foot stomps suggested barn animals and the reels were shrill. In short, it was of a style he writes of in his 1974 analysis of country music.

Conducted for an Apollo troupe known as the Rangers, it is another LRH set piece. Conclusions are drawn from an incisive look at various strains comprising country music, including cowboy laments heard in his youth and ballads he had performed on Washington, DC, radio. In this way, then, sifting and distilling original sounds, came what was described as an authentic form of music that lingered in popular memory.

COUNTRY MUSIC

by L. RON HUBBARD

*I*N LOOKING OVER THE various types of music, including Irish ballads, recent country music albums, I have gotten certain data which is of interest.

There is a whole school of "country western" which is the Roy Rogers / Gene Autry School of Hollywood Soundtrack. Such pieces as "Wagon Wheels," "Ghost Riders" and others were written by Hollywood songwriters in order to fill the tremendous lack of actual pieces in the western catalog. And if you listen to these, you will see that they bear little or no resemblance to actual country music. They are actually an orchestra, usually of the most ordinary type, backing up one or four or five singers who are then singing the Hollywood idea of what they think maybe cowboys should sound like in the idea of audiences. There is very little interest in this, so far as we are concerned, and you might as well forget the whole field of Hollywood western country music.

In researching this, I find that the music written before 1850 is far more melodious, with many more tunes than that written after 1850. Therefore, the heyday of the Old West is actually more or less cancelled out as far as being a source of western music. These songs from 1850 to, let us say, 1890 are of a ballad type. The melodies are quite ordinary, even nonexistent. The moment that you compare these to the pre-1850 period, you are struck with the fact that an entirely different era of music existed. This is mainly due to the existence of minstrels in the Mississippi River steamboat days prior to 1850. Minstrel men were, of course, white men in blackface and their songs bore little or no resemblance to actual Mississippi River colored-population singing. The top writers in this field, of course, include Stephen Foster and his enormous catalog of music. The pre-1850 period contains practically all the forty-niner music. To get the idea of this difference, one only has to think of "Oh, Susanna" and compare it to the dying cowboy to get the idea. It is not that the post-1850 pieces were necessarily only sad. It was that they were slanted toward meaning and words and vocalization whereas the earlier ones had a dependency on music and were actually written by top-flight songwriters like Stephen Foster.

I find that country music, as played modernly, could be greatly improved providing you went back to the source material on the actual instrumentation. The Irish flooded into America and brought with them a fiddle and a certain swing that got into the dance music which was being played in the Middle West from the first days that the Middle West existed. The Irish took it out with them with the railroads, which they built.

Therefore, there are two sources of melody and these consist of the potpourri 1850 songs and the Irish imported songs.

> "I find that country music, as played modernly, could be greatly improved providing you went back to the source material on the actual instrumentation."
>
> —L. Ron Hubbard

There is, as well, a considerable body of music which is simply the dance music which was played in the Middle West, but this again is directly derived from the Irish. The hillbilly bands added their contribution and this was sorted out by Hollywood and made rather popular. But it does not bear very much resemblance to the dance music of the Middle West. This dance music, by the way, was revived by the Ford Foundation and consists of reels and hoedowns which they popularized at the same time that they taught the Middle Western people around Ohio to dance old-time square dances. And there was a whole square dance program by the Ford Foundation. So probably a great deal of this music is in arrangement form. This is a direct source of sheet music for the authentic reels and hoedowns and square dances of the Early West.

Out of all of the bands and types of music, however, the one least pushed and by actual test, the most popular, is the cowboy band.

The cowboy band was a sort of a cross between the Middle Western square dance music and the Mexican band music. Cowboys were not able to carry around very much in the way of instruments and their cowboy bands had a tendency to be very shrill and very sharp. Their drum, for instance, was almost never a snare and consisted mainly in its largest size of something like a military drum except, of course, when you'd see one of these cowboy bands in a rodeo.

The cowboy band is, in itself, more representative of western music and country western than any of the other bands or groups or assemblies.

You, of course, know Herb Alpert's trumpet. Well, this is certainly nothing more than a Mexican trumpet. But this was imported into the cowboy band and the cowboy band was characterized very often by a screaming fiddle and a very shrill trumpet bassed in with a guitar, melodied with a harmonica and given cut with any other instrument which came to hand, which could, of course, be a mandolin or a banjo. This gives a far more authentic sound to western music than most of the other combos which are around. Unfortunately, there is practically no music written for this particular grouping of which I have any knowledge.

Much more interesting is the actual scene of country music and this has been practically lost. I myself have seen this many, many, many years ago and have seen these various dances and have seen singers and the instrumentalists presenting square dances. And they are very remarkable. There is

an awful lot of sole-of-the-foot slapping as opposed to heel beating in jazz or flamenco. It is called stomp or slap. This characterizes the choreography of a hoedown. You can get some idea of the music punctuated with the percussion of slaps when you realize that after a certain riff, why then, there's immediate slap-pop of the flat of the feet followed with another riff and then a stomp-stomp. This dancing approximates horses. And with this type of percussion, you get the reason why I think the square dances were so popular and possibly even why they sort of linger in people's memories. They were very, very active and the percussion was mostly live.

Above
In Palm Springs, California, 1950: a country music aficionado in classic country garb

As Musical Director for Apollo troupes performing big-band standards, Ron inevitably found himself facing that perennial problem of the big-band sound—namely, what is known as instrumental cancellation. In brief, it is the tendency for one instrument to "wipe out" another, regardless of volume. Although bandleaders from Glenn Miller forward devised various remedies, Ron was factually the first to both dissect the problem and define the solution. The result was an altogether unique clarity of sound and all as delineated in Ron's 1974 "Proportionate Sound."

PROPORTIONATE SOUND

by L. RON HUBBARD

THE PROBLEM OF SEPARATION of instruments so they can be separately heard has been largely unsolved in bands and recording.

Study of the subject has brought up certain natural laws apparently not before known.

It has been known, but only as a theory without application, that two cannon fired at each other at the same instant could cancel each other's sound waves and result in silence. I doubt any scientist ever tried it out.

However, the truth is that sound waves *can* cancel sound waves. And this is the basic fact behind proportionate sound.

The laws are:

1. VOLUME of sound, contrary to rock performers and recording engineers, is NOT the controlling factor in instrument separation. You can turn up volume on one instrument and turn down volume on another and *still* get cancellation of sound waves.

2. TIMBRE (tone quality) and PITCH (vibrations per second on the note) are the main points to be used in separating instruments.

3. Instruments of similar timbre and pitch cancel each other's sound waves or one cancels the other.

4. No matter how loud an instrument is played, it may still have trouble in being heard due to cancellation by another.

5. Separation is done by:
   a. Changing the range of the scale between two or more instruments, and
   b. Changing the timbre of the instruments.

6. *Apparent* volume of an instrument can be changed by separating it out by its timbre or pitch from other instruments.

7. Instruments going out of tune can destroy proportionate sound already established.

These laws vigorously applied with full understanding will, with experience, produce clarity of instrument separation never before heard in a musical group.

The voice, for these purposes, is considered an instrument. Voice strain usually occurs through proportionate sound failures or failures to properly mike.

"Wipe" is the expression used to indicate the idea of sound cancellation or lack of separation. "The saxes wiped each other out." "The drum wiped the guitar."

Bass and treble controls are of use in setting proportionate sound.

Microphone changes are the best method of changing timbre in recording.

Microphones of one instrument muddied up by nearby instruments can also mess up proportionate sound as the timbre gets changed.

Direct recording with attention only to meter volume and no attention to proportionate sound (as in 16-track) can produce wipes in the final mix. Therefore proportionate sound is vital to establish before recording. ("Mix" means putting several tracks onto the two stereo or four quad tracks of the final product. It is done through a mixing board.)

Proportionate sound is mandatory if one wants to be heard and if the band instruments are each to be heard.

That Ron would plumb a musical form to the veritable root before expressing himself in that form is yet another LRH hallmark. By way of example comes his 1978 examination of Music and Theater. Tangentially touched on by "mother of modern dance" Martha Graham, the relationship between the two forms is naturally ancient. That Ron further examines performing arts as a cultural barometer and a weather vane of trends makes it doubly fascinating and a signature piece of another order.

MUSIC AND THEATER

by L. RON HUBBARD

THE ACTUAL GENUS OF music and theater is very interesting. If you understand where it really comes from, you get a better understanding of music and theater.

The genus of it is a bunch of hunters, primitive tribes—a hunting society, the most basic-type society. And these guys have been out there in the woods banging deer on the head and getting ducked in cold streams and hand wrestling lions and so forth while the tribe is all sitting at home. The rest of the tribe eat the meat and sometimes they get rather critical about its shortage. So the hunters, unacknowledged, decide to bring the hunt to the village. They usually start in with a *very* primitive, *very* elementary approach—they simply tell the story of today's hunt. And they aren't very verbally or musically inclined. So one of them runs around with his hands over his head being a deer. And the other one chases him around and hits at him with a club or something. Then the deer finally falls in the river and the body floats away.

This advances over a period of time in any given tribe, or in any culture, to a point where they have preserved skins and they have headdresses and they have mock weapons. And from the bang-bang-bang of their sticks trying to drive animals out of the brush, they get the idea that there's rhythm involved in it and then they become more dramatic.

Then they have certain standard hunting exploits which they put in to a standard sort of dance, with standard sort of costumes and a standard sort of rhythm. But you can be very sure that all the way along the line they were working for one thing and that was to make the villagers aware of and interested in hunters.

You get all kinds of things going like this. Almost any village activity will start taking off and dramatizing *its* workload. And they will have sowing songs—how they're sowing the seeds as they get into agricultural societies. They'll have this and they'll have that. They'll have dances and these

Athens, Greece, 1961; photograph by L. Ron Hubbard

Above
Acropolis,
Athens, 1961;
photograph by
L. Ron Hubbard

will have the various rhythms that go along with it. And they'll finally build up a whole repertoire of music and theater peculiar to that tribe or peculiar to that culture.

When a culture goes very bad and very degraded—loses its way in the woods, goes totally technical, isn't really up to anything, starts penalizing its producers and upgrading its nonproducers and goes flip—music and theater lose course. They aren't going in any particular direction, so their music begins to not experience, not express stories.

Their theater is deifying things they should have nothing to do with. You can always tell a culture on the degrade by examining its theater. Aspiration, hope turn up missing. Heroism, gallantry, that sort of thing, disappear. All these things submerge. So you can actually plot the course of an art.

How technical it is or how many helicopters they ride around in have nothing to do with it. It is liable to be on a degrade. The Golden Age of Greece: When they made all their beautiful statues and they were at the peak of their artistic achievement, the rug was already coming out from underneath

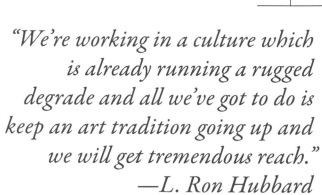

"We're working in a culture which is already running a rugged degrade and all we've got to do is keep an art tradition going up and we will get tremendous reach."
—*L. Ron Hubbard*

Greece and it actually did not have very many more decades to go. So technical achievement can very often ride forward while the dry rot is already setting into the culture.

In trying to put together an art form in this society, that's what you're up against. The normal purposes of art in the culture and so on no longer serve.

But the guys in charge of the arts are the ones who degrade it faster than anybody else and they actually teach a society in this direction. Then all of a sudden somebody brings out *Star Wars,* where everything is heroic and adventurous and so forth, and it makes two hundred million dollars. So you see, if arts would get on the ball, maybe society isn't as late as it thinks.

People still have these sparks and are more anxious to follow those than "It's all hopeless and degraded and we all ought to be on drugs." They still will reach. That's the factor we're working with. We're working in a culture which is already running a rugged degrade and all we've got to do is keep an art tradition going up and we will get tremendous reach.

CHAPTER FOUR

SPACE JAZZ

Space Jazz

IN EARLY 1980, IN CELEBRATION OF HIS FIFTIETH anniversary as a professional writer, Ron returned to the world of popular fiction with his award-winning international bestseller *Battlefield Earth: A Saga of the Year 3000*. Heralded as a masterpiece by critics and readers alike, the 430,000-word epic tells of a Mankind on the verge of extinction following the invasion of a monstrous alien race known as the Psychlos. In an ultimately triumphant response, a classically heroic Jonnie Goodboy Tyler leads a determined band of survivors across a vast and thrilling canvas. The recipient of numerous literary awards, the novel further serves as a model work in several colleges and universities.

Yet *Battlefield Earth* also served as the inspiration for something else—the first-ever musical soundtrack to a book. Aptly entitled *Space Jazz* and reflecting the mood of a futuristic Earth grown primitive following an alien assault, the album offers thirteen LRH compositions based upon significant events and characters from the novel. To best convey the sweep of the saga, the album utilized elements from several genres—from honky-tonk and free-swinging jazz to cutting-edge electronic rock. The result was a wholly new dimension in space opera sound, and what critics declared as a most "auspicious recording debut."

To achieve, in all truth, what was only later approximated, Ron employed a then wholly unexplored device, the Computer Musical Instrument (CMI). Manufactured by Fairlight (which itself had not yet recognized the instrument's full potential), the CMI represented not a new form of synthesizer to replicate sounds, but a means of actually turning natural sounds into notes, so that those sounds *become* the music. The howling wolves are singing the blues, the blast of guns are playing the rhythms and the alien voices are the horn solos. In other words, all manner of previously nonmusical sounds are suddenly "singing" the song and pounding out the rhythm.

Space Jazz, comprising the first literary soundtrack and based on Ron's international bestseller, *Battlefield Earth: A Saga of the Year 3000*

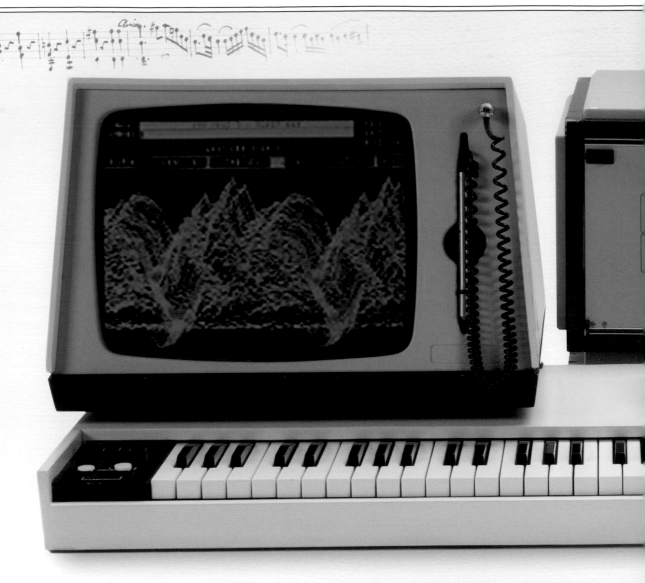

A Note for the Fairlight

"Yours is the fate of pioneers," remarked Ron to studio musicians struggling to harness the Computer Musical Instrument (CMI), and the statement is apt. True, the CMI is now de rigueur. Virtually all rap, for example, essentially qualifies as computer music, while much of what is heard on Top Forty stations likewise employs computers. Yet the summer of 1982 had indeed been a pioneering season for those at work with Ron's Fairlight.

Originally conceived as a novelty and rarely seen beyond experimental laboratories / trade shows, the Fairlight CMI had been generally regarded as a "studio in a box." For suddenly one could digitally record or "sample" any sound and present those sounds through a keyboard as notes. Thus, a dog's bark or cat's meow could be sampled and turned into melody. (In contrast, the synthesizer allowed one only to electronically

imitate a sound and the imitation was never true.) In the beginning, however, talk of the CMI was mostly limited to the sampling of musical instruments (and thus the possibility of a future without live performances or even studio musicians). But as Ron so presciently noted, "The potential of it is not being realized." The CMI "won't put musicians out of work—it will spread music even further."

To determine just how much further music might be spread, his Fairlight was soon transforming a whole array of improbable sounds into musical samples: the thud of rocks, the buzz of drills, the clang of a hoist bucket, the tinkle of bottles and rustling leaves. Conceivably one could even take a revving engine, he explained, "and weave it into percussion and rhythm." Likewise, when scoring his musical rendition of a dancing palomino, recordings of an actual palomino

Above The Fairlight Computer Musical Instrument (CMI)

were fed into the CMI. That is, as he detailed in a note to musicians, "Possibly you may never have seen a horse show with horses dancing. They circle and rear but in this case they circle and tap with their two front hoofs. The melody, in actual fact, adapts to this circling." Slightly more conventionally, if no less imaginative, Ron's Fairlight was also employed to build counter-rhythms from samples of Highland bagpipes and various African tribal instruments.

Needless to say, his employment of the instrument soon captured much national attention as a trend in the making. First publicly heard at the California US Festival, a computer trade show / rock concert, Ron's employment of the Fairlight was generally regarded as a festival highlight. Featured at his *Battlefield Earth* booth, replete with appropriately costumed characters from the novel, the US Festival

provided an apt forum for the release of the world's first computerized soundtrack to a book. Hence, the subsequent newspaper reports: "Movies have soundtracks and, starting in October, so will books." Also clearly evident with the unveiling of his work on the Fairlight was the advent of a whole new era in musical production.

In recognition, then, of all that Fairlight represented as of mid-1982, Ron eventually penned the following salutation to the CMI itself. It reads simply: *"Dear Sir Fairlight: Please have the engineer store on your floppy disc that we have now been properly introduced. I am very glad to make your acquaintance. You have very charming circuits and I am certain that we can co-vibrate to the astonishment and ecstasy of a vast audience. With all praise to your exalted frequencies, consider me your friend."* L. Ron Hubbard ∎

Above
Chick Corea
at the 1982 US
Festival, playing
Ron's Fairlight
Computer
Musical
Instrument

The point is significant even if Ron had been only one of a very few to have recognized it at the time. For whereas the natural sound had long been employed as a musical gimmick—most memorably in the yapping dogs and honking geese used to punctuate the Beatles' *Sgt. Pepper's Lonely Hearts Club Band*—it had never been integrated as *music*. In concise explanation, Ron wrote: "Computer music can incorporate natural sound into musical scales. A bear can growl two thirteen-note octaves. In synthesizer it is NOT a bear growl—it is a synthesizer growl. There is a difference. Natural sound can then be combined with real (not synthesizer) instruments. Add to that the zing of real space opera music and you have a new era of music."

The album reflects exactly that: a new era of music. To convey the drudgery of a forced-labor mining camp, for example, the clatter of mining equipment, transformed into musical phrases, is used to augment the piano, sax and clarinet. "And that was actual mining equipment," explained the album's producer, "meaning we went out and recorded real pickaxes and sledgehammered rocks." While to help convey the typically clamorous saloons of such camps, "we also recorded clinking bar glasses and popping corks from cheap wine bottles."

No less effective are the natural sounds employed to convey an ominous invaders' "March of the Psychlos," including: deepened war chants and the tread of jackboots. While for the Psychlos' laser gun blast, "We combined the crack of a real rifle with the scream of a ricochet and a shrill electric burst from a synthesizer." The net effect is to project the mood and atmosphere of those creatures right into the music, "which even those of us working on the album hadn't quite conceived until we did it."

Similarly, the syncopated tap of hoofs becomes a truly integral part of a song in praise of the hero's horse, while the clamor of real pistons works to convey the mood and atmosphere of the Psychlos' death-dealing "drone." Additionally, interwoven through instrumental melodies are plaintive cries of wolves and coyotes, surging rocket blasts and sighing wind through grass. The net effect is what one critic described as "engaging futuristic sound" with a sense of atmosphere and mood that is almost palpable. For with the CMI in the hands of LRH, one is not hearing either a symphonic suggestion of such sounds, nor even a synthesized approximation. Rather, one is hearing the actual sound transformed into music. Quite literally, then, all that can be imagined as music becomes so. Also quite literally, Ron was at least twenty years ahead of his time.

"We had the Fairlight," explained a musician at work on *Space Jazz,* "but like virtually everyone else, we had no idea of its possibilities until LRH taught us how to use it. We thought in terms of instrumentation and synthesizers, but who would have imagined a natural sound incorporated into the very fabric of a song?"

"With REAL natural sound, in the hands of a true artist," Ron proclaimed in early August 1982, "the Fairlight will revolutionize music and is right now doing so." Of course, he was absolutely correct, and one need only review subsequent sounds for proof. Yet what is ultimately most important is not what followed in the wake of *Space Jazz,* but the album itself.

"I set trends," he very truthfully explained, "not follow them." And the fact is, when he commenced work with the Fairlight in 1982, the CMI had still been an unknown commodity (primarily a novelty among graduate students at Massachusetts Institute of Technology, where musical robots had briefly gained headlines). With Ron's pioneering infusion of artistry, however, all that suddenly changed and *Space Jazz* became not just a glimpse of what would come, but the first realization of "where music is about to go in the future without losing anything of the past." ■

Ron's Musical Research Base

In testament to both Ron's love of music and the scope of his appreciation stands his remarkably extensive personal collection of recordings. Virtually every work of lasting importance has a place in Ron's musical library: from Mozart, Beethoven, Chopin, Brahms and Bach, to Miles Davis, John Coltrane, Bill Evans, Duke Ellington, Ella Fitzgerald and Billie Holiday. In terms of rock, one finds: Pink Floyd, David Bowie, Earth, Wind & Fire, Michael Jackson, the Rolling Stones, the Beatles, Chicago, Deep Purple, Bob Dylan, Jimi Hendrix, the Eagles, Elton John and Frank Zappa, to name but a very few. Along his international shelf are sounds from Russia, Southeast Asia, Turkey, the West Indies, Mexico, Japan, China, Spain, Portugal, Africa, Senegal, Bali, Mongolia and the lower Amazon—to again name just a few.

"What amazed me was not only the quantity of his collection, but the quality," remarked an audiophile enlisted to help catalog the collection. "You simply don't generally see so many great and now rare recordings in one place, including an early Miles Davis album that I've never seen in any audiophile collection."

The fact is, however, Ron did not collect albums for the sake of collecting. Rather, those albums constituted his research base, the window through which he viewed the whole of world music. Those within earshot of his office would routinely hear music from his seriously high-end audio system. And as implied, his tastes were broad—from the latest Top Forty hits to obscure Renaissance madrigals, from experimental rock to '50s pop. Moreover, he was continually recording samples and pertinent comments to help convey ideas to his studio musicians.

In the late 1970s, for example, to broaden the musical scope of musicians at work on LRH compositions, he sent what amounted to an encyclopedia of world music. Within the selection, recalled one of those musicians, "were samples of music types we had not only never heard of, but hadn't even known existed," including obscure strains of the Mongolian war drum, Javanese temple gongs and Balinese chimes. He also included concise descriptions of each type of music and a brief history of the tradition. The point is, he added, "Ron used it all." ∎

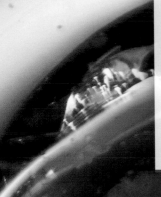

In reply to a young performer grappling with a blues arrangement, Ron offered the following differentiation between musical form and instrumentation. That he further defines a musical message in terms of concept and emotion is key; for therein lies the essence of the art and thus the whole point.

MUSIC FORM AND MUSIC TYPE

by L. RON HUBBARD

B LUES IS A FORM of music expressing despair, which comes from a type of tribal chant in Africa and was imported into the cane and cotton fields as a worker's chant alongside of spirituals. This musical form then reached New Orleans and went up the Mississippi and became the basis of what was called blues. It ceased to be mainly choral and became a solo song sung by a person often called a blues singer.

A music type is not an instrumentalization. The instruments that play it become identified with it in some cases but do not make the music form.

Blues is not something that is only played on a piano even if the modern generation believes so and no matter how many blues tunes you have played on a piano. A piano is an instrument and blues is a musical form.

You have to separate musical forms and musical instrumentation in order to do successful arranging. A musical form is not established by its instrument. It is established by its melody, its met count and its note time value and sometimes by its chording.

Arranging is the act of expressing a musical form and instrumentation is part of arranging.

A form is not an arrangement and an arrangement is not solely instrumentation.

To arrange successfully, one has to have a grip on the musical form one is trying to communicate to an audience. He does an arrangement that will further the form. He chooses instruments in the arrangement to further the arrangement and the form.

To choose a form, one must understand the message one is seeking to convey. A musical message is usually the emotional portion of a concept. All messages are concepts; they are not descriptions of pictures. Concepts, quite ordinarily, have an emotional tone in musical communication. It is this which causes one to choose the musical form and the musical form dictates the arrangement and the arrangement dictates the instruments and all of them add up to a communication of the emotional concept.

DECLARATION OF PEACE

From L. Ron Hubbard's *Space Jazz* album

Reflective of Ron's deeply personal commitment to world peace, lyrics of this song were reprinted on thousands of parchments and bestowed on his behalf to those organizations dedicated to the same ends.

HEAR ME!!

*Out of a hell
of shot and
shell,*

*Out of this
chaos of
contention,*

*Let us bring
peace to
pointless
fight.*

*Why do we court
the whore
called war?*

*Why make of
Earth a
shattered night?*

*There is no
ecstasy
in killing.*

*Love alone
can make
man
willing.*

*So hear me
warriors,
hear me
mothers.*

*There is no
pay in
slaughtered
brothers.*

*Attention, if
your sense
is fair,
heed that which
we now
declare.*

*PEACE! You
races far
and wide.
Peace!
Abandon your
blood-soaked
suicide
and now
abide
in peace!*

*Echo me!
As in your
hearts
you yearn for
love, not
death!*

*PEACE, we
have
declared it.*

*Snarls and strife
must be at end!
In peace alone
can this Earth mend.*

*And now find
ecstasy in
love,
love for Earth,
for all.*

*The gods of
peace have
now spoken.*

OBEY!

CHAPTER FIVE

MISSION EARTH

Mission Earth

AVING PIONEERED THE USE OF NATURAL SOUND and the CMI in terms of jazz, Ron was soon conceiving of another highly innovative musical statement—a progressive rock album based upon his 1984 "An Analysis of Rock Music," wherein he delineated the fundamentals of the form in ways never previously articulated.

The album itself was to constitute another soundtrack—this time for his ten-volume grand satire, the *Mission Earth* series. Telling of a resourceful Royal combat engineer's attempt to foil an alien invasion, *Mission Earth* became an unprecedented publishing event, with all ten volumes successively rising to international bestseller lists. The work was further the recipient of numerous literary awards and received much acclaim for its incisive commentary on a postindustrial world at the brink. Appropriately, then, *Mission Earth,* the album, was to likewise become a highly incisive commentary.

The lyrics themselves are intrinsic to the story and are regularly inserted to break the prose in the manner of a Persian romance (most famously as in Ron's longtime favorite,

The Arabian Nights). "So this actually leaves the book full of lyrics," he explained, "and they are very often stated to be songs." In explanation of how he then composed, generally on his electric organ, he added, "one takes the meter of the lyric, works it out on drums and then fits a melody to that meter."

In further explanation of what he now envisioned, he detailed the use of counter-rhythms—wholly unique to his music and constituting a second rhythm which "would underlie the drum rhythm, usually at lower pitch than the drums. This counter-rhythm would surge exactly in the same way as the rest of the beat."

The result, explained an assistant producer, was a sound so unique that "even those of us involved were unable to initially envision it."

Mission Earth, the album critics described as "a daring conceptual project and an impressive undertaking of tremendous musicianship"

Lyrics and Music by L. Ron Hubbard

"This is a *Mission Earth* album piece—first album—'Joy City.'

"Now, this is a very tricky piece and it's got a lot of gimmicks to it. But first off I'm going to play you an organ arrangement of it just to show you that it goes together as a piece of music."

So began a typical audio cassette of an LRH composition. The use of such cassettes was his unique means of conveying the essence of compositions to studio musicians and arrangers. And those cassettes did, indeed, convey all one needed to know: melody, lyrics, instrumentation and even the employment of natural sounds—all delineated in precise detail.

For example: "Now you will note that this melody has a very dirty bass horn. And this is a fairly dirty bass horn. Now don't get a melodious bass horn, you want a dirty bass horn. This is an interesting trick of reversals whereby you have chorded actions that would normally be in the bass taking place in the treble."

Or: "If you'll notice, there's a first melody, a bass and a bass interlude and then a second melody and another bass interlude and then it goes back to the first melody and the first bass interlude. In other words, there's two types of bass riffs. There's the ones you heard at the very end and then there's the regular bass riffs that just keep going through the piece."

Nor was the flow only one way. When arrangements were complete—and this was true for all Ron's albums—cassettes were sent back to Ron for review. Also included were suggestions for possible orchestration and similar artistic input—as when his musicians suggested the bass and trumpet solos Ron incorporated into the "Mining Song" from the *Battlefield Earth* album. Similarly, when Ron received suggestions that choral and symphonic sections be added to a melody, he replied with a whole new arrangement that, as one musician remarked, "actually went well beyond anything we had imagined—innovative and perfect."

Also routinely heard on the cassettes was Ron at his drum kit to demonstrate a rhythm, as in: "Here is a rhythm, a drum rhythm or a bass rhythm, that can go with it. If you will notice here, there are two sets of drums in use and one is higher than the other. Well, the higher drum is the echo drum and it just goes along like this through the piece."

There were also numerous instructions relating to the employment of such natural sounds as electric air brakes, conductor's voice, slurping straw and buzz of a crowd in his "Joy City" from the *Mission Earth* album; while as a word on the placement of those sounds, he typically included such detailed notes as: "These sound effects occur at each bass riff point between the two melodies."

The net result is exactly the sum of all that Ron delineated in such cassettes: Three entire albums, dozens of film scores and a whole catalog of songs that effectively begin with "Here is the melody…" ∎

"L. Ron Hubbard has done considerable research into rock music. He had written quite a bit on the history of rock and its development. I had not been aware that he knew who I was or that he followed the rock scene. It was certainly an honor and a privilege to work with him."
—Edgar Winter, Rock Musician

Above
Blues-rock legend Edgar Winter at work on *Mission Earth*

Yet gradually laying down Ron's counter-rhythms and heavy orchestration, "it slowly began to dawn on us that we were creating a whole new sound with a full symphonic backdrop to a surging rock ensemble." The album further paints atmospheric scenarios in truly imaginative ways. Take the title track, for instance, wherein a troupe of Turkish percussionists—discovered performing in a Los Angeles Middle Eastern restaurant—supplied a fully unique counter-rhythm to the heavy main beat of the song itself. ("I'm certain those percussionists had no concept of how their work would finally turn out, but if ever one wanted an authentic sound—those people supplied it.")

In apt description of the innovations Ron introduced in the *Mission Earth* album, one newspaper's reviewer wrote of a "music, which spans the gamut of busy orchestrated arrangements, to bluesy '40s jazz, to contemporary pop...dominated by creatively programed keyboards. Rooting it all down is heavy percussion and a powerful upfront mix on the drums."

The album also, of course, features Ron's intricate rock melodies to virtually paint scenes portrayed.

To help carry all to fruition, the album further features celebrated sax, keyboards and vocals of blues-rock legend Edgar Winter. Renowned for smash hits "Frankenstein" and "Free Ride," with their early employment of the synthesizer, Winter rightly described *Mission Earth* as both a return to rock's primal roots and yet highly experimental. Working from Ron's detailed audio cassettes (see "Lyrics and Music by L. Ron Hubbard"), Winter also served as arranger. In particular reference to his work in that capacity was what he described as Ron's unique match of melodic tone with the emotional content of lyrics and, of course, "Ron's technical insight of the recording process was outstanding." No less remarkable, Winter went on to explain, was Ron's delineation of counter-rhythm in rock, "which was nothing short of phenomenal, particularly inasmuch as it had then been entirely unexplored and only later heard in the African-based rhythms of Paul Simon's work, some five years after Ron's analysis."

What Winter would most generally discuss, however, was the album's inherent message of planetary concern. Reflecting L. Ron Hubbard's lifelong focus on key cultural issues, including rampant pollution and drug abuse,

Mission Earth, the album, legitimately stands as the decade's most potent musical statement for environmental reform. Its environmental anthem, "Cry Out," was not only adopted by Friends of the United Nations in the name of ecological reform, but became the rallying cry for a worldwide Earth Day celebration. The subsequent "Cry Out" video further enjoyed national airplay on Earth Day, while the "Cry Out" single was likewise heard on national radio. Appropriately, all profits from the song were donated for the reprint of the *Personal Action Guide for the Earth* booklet on behalf of the United Nations Environment Programme.

"A daring conceptual project and an impressive undertaking of tremendous musicianship, matched with ultraslick production" critics declared of L. Ron Hubbard's *Mission Earth* album, and the description is apt. For with innovative under-rhythm and computerized percussion the likes of which had never been heard, here indeed was music described as a genuine "orchestral adventure." ∎

CRY OUT

Marching Song of the Protesters
From L. Ron Hubbard's *Mission Earth* album

Adopted as the rallying cry for environmental groups the world over, this song became the anthem of the 20th anniversary of Earth Day International and so earned proclamations from cities world over. A single was produced for the benefit of the United Nations environmental cause.

Once it was a very nice planet
A home for those of us who care
But there are fools in high places
Who foul the sea and air
They dump the land with toxic waste
They spill the sea with oil
They poison plant and animal
And irradiate the air and soil

Chorus:

We've got to, Cry out, Protest
Object, Be heard
Day in, day out
This fight must never rest
It's time to save the world
Cry out, Protest
Object, Be heard
Let's raise a shout

Make this our common quest
To build a better world

And that's not the worst,
The deadly burst of radiation fission looms
Threatening to send the lot of us
To our collective dooms
To hell with those whose carelessness
In pollution is expressed
To hell with force politics
Where victory is only death

Chorus

This planet once was so alive
And nature bloomed in every spot
The time to save the earth is now
'Cause it's the only home we've got

Chorus

E-METER INSTRUCTION FILM 1
MAN, THE UNFATHOMABLE
L. RON HUBBARD
EM 2 THE TONE SCALE L. RON HUBBARD
EM 2A TONE SCALE DRILL FILM L. RON HUBBARD
EM 3 THE HISTORY OF THE E-METER L. RON HUBBARD
EM 4 HOW THE E-METER WORKS L. RON HUBBARD
EM 5 HOW TO SET UP A SESSION AND AN E-METER L. RON HUBBARD
EM 6 FALSE TA L. RON HUBBARD
EM 7 BODY MOTION READS L. RON HUBBARD
EM 8 ESTIMATING CASE CONDITIONS BY TESTS AND THE E-METER L. RON HUBBARD
EM 9 E-METER READS L. RON HUBBARD
EM 9A E-METER READS DRILL FILM L. RON HUBBARD
EM 10 PC INDICATORS L. RON HUBBARD
EM 10A PC INDICATORS DRILL FILM L. RON HUBBARD
Man, The Unfathomable
by L. Ron Hubbard
Confessional TRs
by L. Ron Hubbard
Evolution of a Science
by L. Ron Hubbard
Thesis
bbard
STACCATO
A TEMPO

TR 3 — THE ART OF COMMUNICATION — L. RON HUBBARD
TR 4 — TRs 0 TO 4 — L. RON HUBBARD
TR 5 — WHY TRs? — L. RON HUBBARD
TR 6 — USE OF A DOLL IN AUDITING AND TRs — L. RON HUBBARD
TR 7 — UPPER INDOC TRs — L. RON HUBBARD
TR 8 — START, CHANGE AND STOP — L. RON HUBBARD
TR 9 — THE AUDITOR'S CODE — L. RON HUBBARD
TR 10 — ASSISTS — L. RON HUBBARD
TR 11 — TONE 40 ASSESSMENT — L. RON HUBBARD
TR 12 — THE SOLO AUDITOR — L. RON HUBBARD
TR 13 — THE SESSION — L. RON HUBBARD
TR 14 — CONFESSIONAL TRs — L. RON HUBBARD
TR 15 — THE DIFFERENT TR COURSES AND THEIR CRITICISM — L. RON HUBBARD
TR 16 — THE ULTIMATE TRs – BEINGNESS — L. RON HUBBARD

Scoring for the Screen

A musical score for a film, Ron long maintained, is a piece of music in its own right, but with particular qualifications. In the first place, the musical soundtrack, by definition, is intended to augment the pictures. In that regard, as he explained, "It could be likened to an interpreter who, standing slightly to the side, tells the audience what to *feel* about what they are seeing." Consequently, "One should not get the idea that cine music is secondary, for it has no small role in films and related subjects. It establishes and engenders the emotional reaction of the audience to the pix. In other words, it is actually influencing audience emotional response to the film."

His own compositions are exactly that: wonderfully memorable melodies to precisely forward the filmic message. Moreover, the L. Ron Hubbard film score melody was perfectly adaptable to any musical style, and could thus be reiterated through the film for unity. In all, he scored music for twenty-two Scientology training and promotional films, all underscoring the fact that, as he put it: "To grasp the role of music in cine, one first has to understand and accept the fact that music, in itself, is capable of communication." ■

As noted, each of Ron's musical creations represented a specific musical genre. From his years aboard the Apollo came Star Sound, while Space Jazz was unique for its use of natural sound and computer music.

For an insight into what made the Mission Earth album so special, rock legend Edgar Winter was to comment, "Up until my work on Mission Earth, I had not been aware that Ron had a particular interest in rock music. But when I read his research, I was amazed at what I found. Ron analyzed the history and development of rock music and came up with the exact formula of what makes a hit rock song. It was unlike anything I'd ever read before and made total sense to me." The following, then, is Ron's 1984 analysis and study of the "ins and outs" of rock, forming the basis of the Mission Earth album.

AN ANALYSIS OF ROCK MUSIC

by L. Ron Hubbard

THE FOLLOWING IS AN analysis of rock music. There are probably as many opinions about what is rock as there are tastes in music. And you are perfectly at liberty to disagree with any of the following, as it is simply a summary of what makes rock rock and you may be a devotee of rock or abhor it. But we are not dealing with taste here or preference. We are simply dealing with a very generalized analysis of a type of music.

History

The origins of rock are differently assigned by different experts on the subject. They do seem to agree that it originated as a genre in 1956 or '57.

Rock seems to be a joining of at least two streams of music: One stream comes from the West Virginia hills in the form of ballads. West Virginia music, however, traces directly back to the "buskers"—the street singers of England, who covered themselves with buttons and were prominent in central London two or three hundred years ago. The bulk of the songs you find in West Virginia originate as busker songs with the difference that the buskers sang the melodies much prettier, in that they introduced minors. By the time the Scots and English, with that music, settled in the hills of West Virginia, their treatment of the same melodies which had been in minor chords took on the form of major chords. The other stream would seem to be from New Orleans, where jazz had gained a beachhead in America. Jazz actually comes from Africa on the route of the slave trade through Martinique and then to New Orleans. This music flowed up the Mississippi, often taking on the tinge of spirituals.

These two streams, possibly colored by others, arrived at centers of music, one of which was Nashville.

Rock is not a pure genre, in the sense that it mushes together several real genres. *But* I can assure you that rock has been on the track almost as long as there has been music.

Surveys

The following survey was recently conducted on the music-buying public. While the percentages which were the top percentage of the answers would not seem to be a majority of percentages, the other percents of answers were miniscule and one would have to assume that this is a dominant opinion as follows:

1. Q. What musical direction would you like to see rock and roll take next?
    A. Back-to-basics, old rock and roll, early '50/'60s. (16.7%)

2. Q. How do you feel rock and roll today could be improved?
    A. Less hard rock, away from punk. (30.0%)

3. Q. What makes rock different from other types of music?
    A. Beat, rhythm. (31.7%)

4. Q. Why is the beat such an important part of rock and roll?
    A. Makes you dance, move. (35.0%)

5. Q. Why do you think so many rock songs are about love?
    A. Everybody can relate to it. (48.3%)

6. Q. What does rock and roll do for you?
    A. Makes me feel good, puts me in a good mood. (30.0%)

The above would seem to indicate that the music-buying public at least has some agreement on what rock is and actually it is not too bad a description.

Charts

A rather long-term study of charts indicates that record sales of rock are overpoweringly greater than that of any other type of music. It has the lion lion's share of sales.

At the same time this is occurring, the music industry is going downhill on a toboggan slide. It reportedly is really in the doldrums. A review of the charts of bestsellers at this time reveals a few groups.

Below
Setúbal, Portugal, while recording the Apollo Stars, 1974

And a review of their cassettes does not, hold your hat, reflect very much adherence to the genre. It is an oddity about these top-of-the-chart groups that these days they seem to appear and disappear, the bulk of them, with considerable speed. One could rationalize this by saying that public taste is fickle, but this is countered, on analysis, by the fact that the records of old rock stars continue to sell and heavily. In other words, one could assume that these very modern groups have begun to depend upon freak impact or appearance rather than on music or adherence to the genre. Of course this is open to a great deal of analysis and other opinion, but the survey quoted above would seem to agree, as 30 percent of the music buyers in question 2 demonstrated dissatisfaction. And the number of bankruptcies in the music business seem to agree with it also.

Above
At a radio station with the Stars on the Canary Islands

Stars

One could go into a lengthy discussion of various rock stars, but it would begin to lead back to the Beatles and Presley. And their records are hot sellers even today.

But this point can be made concerning the beginning of careers of the real stars of rock. It has been observed that the real giant stars—notably Elvis Presley and the Beatles—burst into huge, long-lasting fame at an exact point in their careers: They used orchestral backup. Presley, for instance, became a "here-to-stay" star on a nationwide TV show backed up by the NBC orchestra. And the Beatles were actually playing and recording classical backed up by an orchestra even though you see the four of them out there in front. Their producer, George Martin, was a classical man who also did most of the arranging. (He was called the "fifth Beatle.") From this a point can be concluded: that rock stars and rock groups who back up with an orchestral have lasting duration. This is a new observation arrived at by somebody who is a student of this sort of thing and it seems to check out. Three or four electric guitars are not the background which make lasting rock stars. Thus one can conclude that successful rock employs not just a twanging gimmick or two, but a whole, well-skilled orchestra as backup. This is true of singers and music in other fields: You should hear the orchestral backup in terms of numbers and arrangements of Rudy Vallee, Bing Crosby, Frank Sinatra, etc. Since the focal point of the public is on some star, this tends to get overlooked, but it is not basically overlooked by the public.

The point here is that three or four guys with electric instruments get beat out every time by somebody with full orchestral backup.

Choral also enters into this scene. The Presley use of choral was amazing and today choral is extensively used in rock backup. This is, actually, the spiritual stream which seems to have entered into modern rock.

One can conclude that successful and lasting rock music has (a) heavy and numerous orchestral backup which sometimes includes choral and (b) is well arranged.

An Analysis

A study of the rock genre, as it is modernly and even historically performed, shows that it lacks in the aggregate the following (with exceptions here and there, which exceptions have actually made stars):

1. Melody,

2. Articulation,

3. Plan,

4. Arrangement (aside from a few spectacular pieces),

5. Message,

6. Trained voices, and

7. Expert instrumentalists.

Where some pieces included one or more of these it has been successful.

What rock has is:

    a. Physiological impact,

    b. Chords,

    c. Beat, and

    d. A feeling of excitement (or hysteria).

And it is to be commented on that current rock even lacks some one or more of the (a) to (d).

Reviewing some of the more all-time successful pieces demonstrates that they did have some of (1) to (7) and had (a) to (d).

The above, however, as an analysis, gives you a key to what could become very successful rock. All you have to do is combine (1) to (7) with (a) to (d) and you should have it made.

Physiological Impact

This is accomplished by an accented beat or a surge in rhythmic fashion. It is an actual physical thud repeated.

It is to be remarked, as an aside, that the modern mixing engineer, with his frail equipment, uses what is called a limiter to keep from being blown off the board and he is actually killing the physiological impact. In other words, on albums and so forth you don't hear the surge to the degree that it is played and it is often not even played to that surge. Seldom being musicians, the sound engineers have not really worked out a way to handle this. It is actually quite simple: You just carry the level of the program 2 or 3 decibels down from 0 on your VU meter or as low as even minus 7 decibels and let the physiological impact of the drums, etc., shoot it up to 0. The rest of the program would fall below minus 4 or minus 7, or whatever, and for the usual playback machines could go as low as minus 15. In this way, physiological impact would be preserved.

Chords

Most rock songs are composed just of chords such as you find in a guitar book. They take a chord progression and work with it. The probable reason they do this is that it is actually harder to put beat or impact into a melody. One can take chords and bang the guitars and drums at the same time and produce a surge. It requires a lot more expertise to do this with band instruments in melody. Their singers too, in most cases, are not following any melody because they are introducing shouts and it is easiest to do this by just going up and down some chord progression. It would take a much more expert singer to throw real impact in the melody. (The singing you hear on rock is really not part and parcel of rock at all—there is no reason for somebody to sound like he is being lynched just to produce excitement. Presley rather pushed this into the scene heavily, but it is not really part and parcel of rock at all. It takes a very skilled singer to sing with excitement and actually sing properly.)

Beat

The key to rock is really beat. The dictionary defines *beat* as "Music. A regular pulsation; the basic unit of musical time. The measured sound of verse; rhythm."

What makes actual rock rock is by accenting the beat. The definition of *accent* is "Music. Emphasis or stress on a note or chord."

Most rock is in 4/4 time, which is to say, four quarter notes to the measure. The met count of rock runs between 120 and 130 with a few exceptions. Certain of those quarter notes is stressed or made louder or accented in a continuing pattern—with the addition of breaks, etc.

The accents of rock are various but are all one of the following:

(In the following examples the whole numbers represent maximum volume surge and the dashes represent normal volume of the beat.)

1	—	—	—
1	—	3	—
—	2	—	4
—	—	—	4

This is not all the beats possible for rock. There could also be:

—	2	3	—
1	—	—	4
1	2	—	—
—	—	3	4

There is a possible variation even in all the above: In any of the places of a normal volume, one could have a ½ *accent,* which would be defined as "something halfway between normal rhythm and the volume of the surge." One could also have a ¼ accent and a ¾ accent or even a ⅓ accent and a

⅔ accent. Of course, if they were all accented, you would have no surge. But there are variations of patterns possible, such as the following:

I

⅓ accent

⅔ accent

Full accent

   or

4

⅔

⅓

—

This would give you a sort of gradient surge up or a gradient surge down. And there could be other variations which give actual surges.

In examining rhythm, I recently invented what you could call "counter-rhythm," which would underlie the drum rhythm, usually at lower pitch than the drums. This counter-rhythm would surge exactly in the same way as the rest of the beat.

This accent is repetitive. This is done usually by hitting the principal drum at the quarter-note point being accented or by adding a bass at that point or some other such mechanism. A very expert drummer, of course, can change the volume of sound on the same drum.

It is with this surge that physiological impact is produced.

Excitement

The genre, rock, has an emotional target, in most cases, of excitement. Most modern rock groups, however, forget that they are dealing with sound and perform in an excited way while not really playing in an excited way. But the real stars could produce a feeling of excitement. They do this by various mechanisms, but I assure you they haven't actually really touched the mechanisms available. Presley rather set the pace and left his brand on rock singing, but that doesn't mean that everyone has to sing like Presley—a long way from it.

Excitement consists of the emotional response of something of great interest happening or about to happen, but excitement can be produced simply by successions of notes and melodic sounds. In trying to do this, singers lose articulation and who knows what they're singing about. In other words, they are not well-enough trained to sing excitedly and articulately and substitute for it getting strangled. It takes real skill to shout, for instance, and still have somebody understand what you're shouting about and still shout melodiously. They manage it in opera. They managed it exceptionally well in light opera. But those guys had trained voices.

Summary

The conclusion of the analysis is that if one combined points (1) to (7) above with (a) to (d) above, one would really produce some stellar, popular music.

But it should be added that such music would have to be handled well from beginning to end. Proportionate sound would have to be known about and used in arranging, recording and mixing. (This is the technique of "separation"—as it is known in the recording industry. Without it, one gets instruments wiped out and gets clashing and mushes.)

It is agreed that it takes real expertise to bring off all those points in a piece of music, but it can be done.

An analysis of rock as it is being performed contemporarily shows that it is *not* being done.

Thus the door is wide open to a new era of popular music.

Organs

The primary instrument upon which Ron composed was the electronic organ. Whether composing scores for new Scientology films or songs and melodies for an album, this was his instrument of choice. Keenly conscious of innovations in design and construction, his organs were always, quite simply, cutting edge. If it was new, he was interested in it; and if it would enhance his work, he obtained it. ■

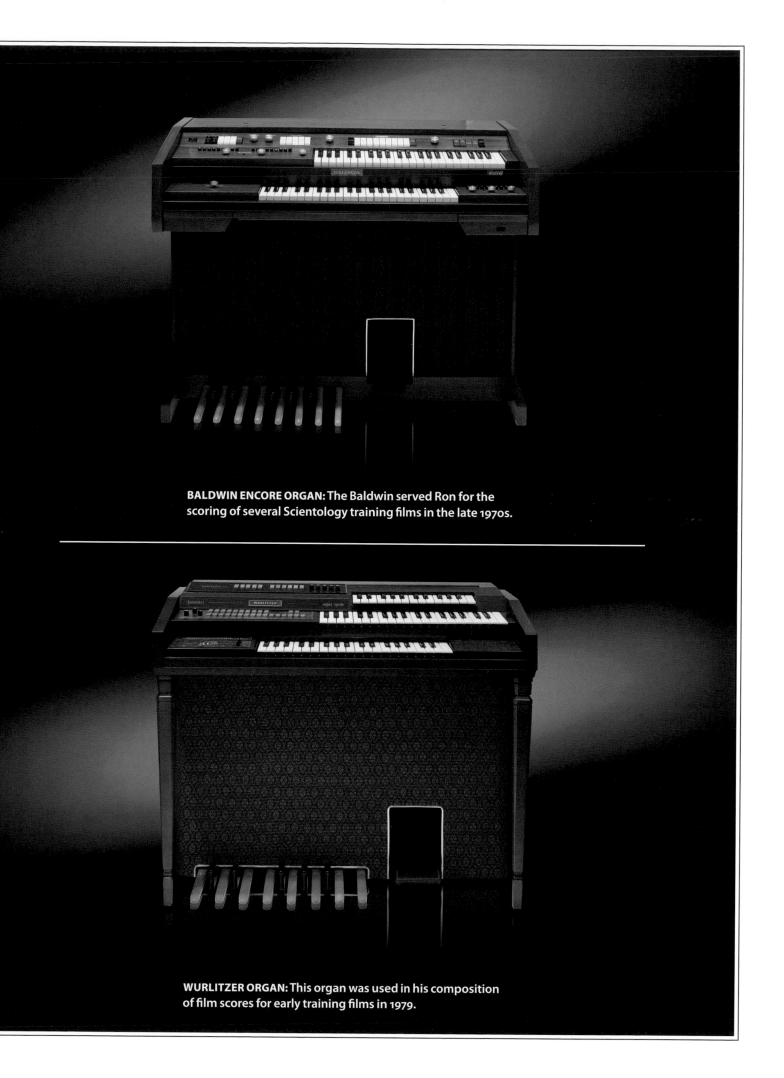

BALDWIN ENCORE ORGAN: The Baldwin served Ron for the scoring of several Scientology training films in the late 1970s.

WURLITZER ORGAN: This organ was used in his composition of film scores for early training films in 1979.

HAMMOND ORGAN: One of the most popular electronic organs, Ron's Hammond was also used in his scoring of instructional and dissemination films during 1979 and 1980. Of the Hammond, he wrote: "This keyboard has a remarkable potential in altering the timbre of sound with its slides. One can actually even use those slides to separate a sound out or to prevent it from wiping." (See "Proportionate Sound," on page 49.)

KAWAI ORGAN: Ron used this instrument to score the music for audio recordings of his Ron's Journal of 9 May 1981. The Kawai was also used for film soundtrack composition, and the songs for his *Space Jazz* album. "A great church organ," he proclaimed. "It also has a small set of slides to change the timbre of its voices. And it has another device which, on some settings, can control the attack and decay of a sound as well as the speed of strum on such a thing as a mandolin."

YAMAHA FX-3: "This is a fantastic box of tricks," Ron said of this organ. In particular he pointed to the FX-3's "absolutely superb trumpets, tubas, trombones, violins and many other instrumental sounds." The FX-3 was a triumph of electronic organ construction and subsequent organs by the same manufacturer never lived up to the quality of this instrument. Indeed, it stands as the premier electronic organ of all time. Consequently, the FX-3 still stands in Ron's composing room. Also shown is Ron's recording equipment, which was all custom-built to his exact specifications. Such was used to record his various musical compositions as well as instructional notes to musicians and arrangers. (See article "Lyrics and Music by L. Ron Hubbard," on page 74.)

Composing on the Road

In L. Ron Hubbard's *Mission Earth,* the central hero, Jettero Heller, travels across America in a customized "land yacht." In fact, Ron was writing of his own land yacht—a customized Blue Bird motor home in which he took to the road through central and northern California. To continue his musical composition, a separate trailer was specially outfitted

as part of his caravan. Pictured here is that mobile composition room, containing a scaled-down version of his composition and recording facilities, including his Yamaha FS-500. In fact, it was in this mobile composition recording room that Ron composed the songs for his *Mission Earth* album and *The Road to Freedom.* ∎

Synthesizers

BALDWIN SYNTHA SOUND: Acquired in 1975 and immediately proving an instrument of choice. In point of fact, this one is the synthesizer prompting Ron to describe the Baldwin line as "invaluable."

ARP AXXE: One of the first "mini synthesizers" that amply served an itinerant L. Ron Hubbard beyond 1979.

KORG POLY-800: A gift from acclaimed jazz keyboardist Chick Corea, the Korg Poly-800 was a particularly popular synth in the early 1980s.

PROPHET-T8: Purchased for Ron's composition room in the early 1980s and also used in the L. Ron Hubbard Music Studio.

YAMAHA DX7 SYNTHESIZER: In 1984, intrigued with what he had heard of the new synthesizers, Ron ordered a search and test of all leading models. The Yamaha DX7 was found to be the ideal instrument for his composition needs. At the time, however, the DX7 was unavailable within the United States and so arrangements were made to purchase the instrument directly from the Japanese manufacturer.

ROLAND JUNO-60: Also acquired for Ron's composition room, the Roland served musicians through the recording of the album, *Mission Earth* in 1985. ∎

The Music Room

containing the complete collection of
L. Ron Hubbard's musical instruments.

The L. Ron Hubbard Studio and legendary Massenburg mix board, one of two in the world and without equal

CHAPTER SIX

The L. Ron Hubbard MUSIC STUDIO

The L. Ron Hubbard
Music Studio

Constructed in accord with all Ron provided in the name of quality recording, is the L. Ron Hubbard Music Studio. In a word, it is the perfect recording environment, and indisputably stands as the finest such facility in the world. From physical design to equipment configuration and installation standards, from acoustics allowing

for the reproduction of exact sound qualities to the singularly finest mix board—here is a studio with an unmatched reputation for technical fidelity.

Intrinsic to that fidelity is a physical design in absolutely strict accord with Ron's delineation of sound behavior—what best reflects sound, what best records it, how it is best channeled and relayed. In consequence, here is a studio that offers a "building within a building," each room set on its own "floating" concrete slab (replete with separate walls and ceiling) to ensure no sound transmission during recording. The net result is a facility to perfectly capture the true sound of any voice or instrument without

alteration.... Which is to say, all a performer is capable of delivering will purely and faithfully make it to the recording.

In testament to exactly that comes premier acoustics engineer, Paul S. Veneklasen. The first modern name in environmental sound, and the man behind acoustical interiors in some of America's finest performing arts facilities, Mr. Veneklasen proclaimed: "This studio is the best I've ever seen in all my fifty years in the field of sound recording—the best, bar none!"

Once sound is recorded, the L. Ron Hubbard Music Studio provides the artist with yet another tool that is, quite simply, the best in

the world: the handmade George Massenburg mix board. One of only two such mix boards ever constructed, the Massenburg has become a legendary piece of equipment. It was one of the first fully computer-automated mix boards, and Ron's is the larger of the two. Today, it has become known as the premier mixing board, tenaciously sought by studios everywhere, because it has no equal.

Similarly reflecting Ron's singular emphasis on quality are his microphones—legitimately among the finest ever made, and collected from around the world through his many years of recording work.

Even to the smallest details, that quality is uncompromised—as in Ron's patented "Bleeder Bar." A device attached to a tape recorder, it is designed to remove or "bleed"

excess electrons from a recorded tape just as it crosses the recording head.

What all such details add up to is precisely what was most important to Ron: an ideal atmosphere for artistic performance. Specifically to that end—and in contrast to the generally impersonal feel of commercial facilities that look more like a sauna than a studio—the L. Ron Hubbard Music Studio is truly a place that replicates the world of live performance. The philosophy behind such an atmosphere is simple: Ron knew only too well that the musician expresses his greatest creativity in a live performance. Thus, his studio was expressly designed to simulate an actual theater where the performer *is* on stage. In consequence, Ron's studio resembles a stage. Looking from the studio into the control room, one sees a tapestry

of admiring listeners. The performance area is ringed with stage lights and curtains, while one enters from theater wings—all to offer a sense of *that moment* to bring out the best in an artist.

The net result of all that lies within Ron's studio, including both its design and equipment, is nothing less than the benchmark of sound recording as a whole. In that regard, the L. Ron Hubbard Music Studio is a direct reflection of all L. Ron Hubbard stood for as a Music Maker: his codification of musical basics, his understanding of music as communication, his technical expertise precisely and, above all, his love of music and musicians everywhere. ∎

Above
The LRH Music Studio, designed to simulate what generally brings out the best in any musician—a *live* performance

Sound, Panels and Chambers

When capturing the intricate sounds of musical instruments or the human voice, the goal is to record the complete sound spectrum generated, without alteration. To exactly that end, Ron recommended a nonreverberant room, a neutral space, to produce this sound purely and unaffectedly.

The underlying theory is simple enough. Each instrument or vocal performer emanates sounds in complex ways from numerous points, not simply from a single source. Although one might imagine that numerous microphones would effectively capture those sounds, such is not the case. Indeed, an array of mikes would yield an array of unwanted acoustic anomalies.

The L. Ron Hubbard Music Studio ingeniously handled the problem with unique reflective panels constructed of Lexan. The convex surfaces of these panels are engineered to reflect the entire sound evenly over the entire audio spectrum. With the proper placement in the acoustic environment, all subtleties, beauty and character of the instrument or performer become available for capture by the microphone—a striking advance in modern recording.

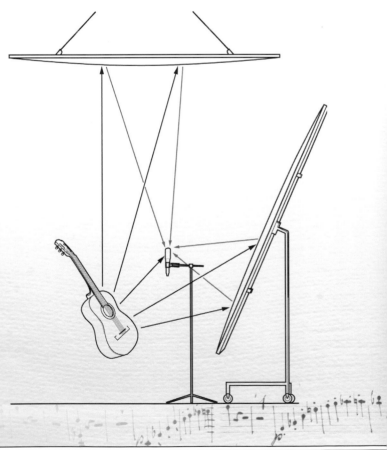

Echo Chambers

The L. Ron Hubbard Music Studio further features specially constructed echo chambers to enhance and enliven the musical experience. A listener hears sound generated from a source that is naturally embellished by the acoustic reflections of the environment surrounding that source. For that reason symphonies are performed at venues that enhance the musical experience. An echo chamber accomplishes something similar. It is expressly constructed and appointed with high-fidelity speakers to create a reverberation that enhances the music. These chambers are acoustically tuned to provide a pleasant and spacious effect.

Choralizer

The Choralizer is a one-of-a-kind device employing a pair of moving microphones in an echo chamber to provide not only reflective enhancement, but a subtle pitch shifting from the Doppler effect. The result is the wonderfully vibrant and rich sound heard on many a recording from the L. Ron Hubbard Music Studio. Deploying an astonishing arrangement of belts and pulleys, the moving pattern of the microphones never repeats. Mr. Paul S. Veneklasen conceived and executed the design of this engineering marvel, and the technicians at the LRH studio helped realize its construction and utilization. ■

The Art and Science of Recording and Relaying Sound

"Over the years I have undertaken to make available, where needed, precise and useful data on the subject of operation of sound equipment. I do this from the position of a skilled recordist and real time and mix line mixer."—L. Ron Hubbard

To cite a few particulars: Beyond 1950, Ron particularly devoted himself to quality recording and copying for the preservation and distribution of his lectures on Dianetics and Scientology. In addition to miking, recording and mixing Apollo Star music through the early 1970s, he is still remembered as the line engineer *par excellence* for southern Florida radio performances of local church choirs and gospel groups. With his 1978 formation of a unit for the production of Scientology films and music, he eventually authored volumes on the operator side of audio. In consequence came the much-talked-about sound technology known today as *Clearsound* and exclusively utilized by Golden Era Productions for a quality of recording and reproduction virtually surpassing all industry standards. Yet also within Ron's instructional materials

for recording and relaying sound is a delineation of acoustic principles for an *understanding* of sound…and therein lies the basis from which he provided that precise and useful data on the operation of sound equipment.

It is found nowhere else, and begins with his description of sound—not as a generally misconceived wave, but as an energy force unto itself. That is, "Sound travels because vibrating molecules make the surrounding molecules vibrate at a similar rate. When you graph different pitches—vibrations per second—of sound, you get something which looks like a wave. But it isn't a wave, it's just an energy force which sets atmosphere molecules into vibration which then causes agitation of nearby molecules which in turn communicate the vibration to other molecules and you get a traveling vibration."

What such an explanation has to do with sound recording is, frankly, a lot. For following from a grasp of sound *behavior* in terms of molecular vibration comes all he provided for selecting and operating equipment.

That is to say, "Each different item, line, component or whatever in a recording, mixing or transferring process has a certain exact *operator* purpose and does certain exact things to the vibrations."

To ensure those things were done exactly right, Ron examined and tested scores of components singly and in combination. Where necessary—as in a not-quite-noiseless, but otherwise excellent recorder—he modified internal circuitry. He also tested sound characteristics in every pertinent way—mapping distinguishing qualities on oscilloscopes to determine what sounds will habitually cancel out others. He similarly examined sound behavior as regards wall and ceiling surfaces. (Although distortion from the echo effect of parallel walls was generally known, he determined all-too-common plaster likewise distorts sound, as do many common interior wall paints.)

There is still more on equipment utilization and operation: selecting and placing microphones to "balance" sound in accord with his laws of proportionate sound, ensuring no piece of equipment is fed a level of sound (either too high or too low) for which it must compensate and so may distort, always guaranteeing that one machine sounds exactly like another and that what comes out of a line sounds exactly like what went in. Finally, and given instruments do not always register sudden shifts of sound quality or volume, Ron further provided drills. They are drawn from Scientology principles and specifically aimed at curing "quality deafness" and training operators to listen at different frequencies for that ultimate test of sound quality—*hearing it*.

Needless to say, the sum of all Ron offers for recording and handling quality sound returns us to his overall definition of art as the *quality* of communication. It also perfectly dovetails with all else he presented in the name of enhancing musical communication. Hence, his summary pronouncement on this art and science of relaying music to excite, lull, thrill or enthrall: *"The name of the game is sound."* ■

MICROPHONES: Ron's cherished collection of microphones is legitimately among the finest in the world. It includes such utterly rare makes and models as the Neumann U 47s, U 48s, M 49, M 250 and numerous vintage AKG C 12s—meaningless names to the layman, but tantamount to a Stradivarius in the eyes of recording professionals and astute musicians. For although long since out of production, these microphones offer a warmth and clarity that has never been wholly replicated.

CHAPTER SEVEN

The Road to FREEDOM

SIDE 1

THE ROAD TO
FREEDOM

AND

THE ROAD TO
FREEDOM

AND FRIENDS

THE ROAD TO
FREEDOM

1. THE ROAD TO FREEDOM
2. THE WAY TO HAPPINESS
3. THE WORRIED BEING
4. THE EVIL PURPOSE
5. LAUGH A LITTLE
6. THE GOOD GO FREE
7. WHY WORSHIP DEATH?
8. MAKE IT GO RIGHT
9. THE ABC SONG
10. L'ENVOI
THANK YOU FOR LISTENING

CLEARSOUND
COMPACT
DISC

AND FRIENDS

THE ROAD TO
FREEDOM

AND FRIENDS

The Road to
Freedom

GIVEN THAT SO MUCH OF WHAT L. RON HUBBARD accomplished musically depended upon tools drawn from his development of Scientology, it is only fitting he would next present an album comprising a Scientology musical statement. That album, featuring performances by Scientology luminaries is aptly entitled *The Road to Freedom*.

Essentially religious music in Scientology style, *The Road to Freedom* represents the culmination of all Ron pioneered as Music Maker. The album offers ten L. Ron Hubbard compositions to convey essential Scientology truths for what he described as "wide public acquaintance with what Scientology is all about." If the result does not immediately match preconceived ideas of devotional music, it is because Scientology does not require blind devotion. Its truths are self-evident and not a matter of faith. *The Road to Freedom,* then, does not preach; it informs.

Central to its message is the very key Scientology datum that, as inherently spiritual beings, our actual capabilities are far in excess of what anyone has allowed us to believe. In that regard, and particularly when viewed *vis-à-vis* the traditionally devotional religious

hymn, *The Road to Freedom* becomes a powerful affirmation of who we are and what we can potentially accomplish.

The case in point is "Why Worship Death?" In opposition to the traditional requiem wherein death is seen as a terrifying doom, Ron's "Why Worship Death?" is cheerfully defiant. After all, what is the passing of a body to a spiritual being who is absolutely certain of his own immortality? It is, as the song proclaims, *"a sham, a curtain of forgetfulness instilled as a memory jam."*

In the same uniquely optimistic vein is "Laugh a Little," to remind us that our contentment and well-being is entirely within us and "Make It Go Right" to remind us that we can, indeed, prevail over all life's barriers. Also included is a musical explanation of L. Ron Hubbard's nonreligious moral code,

L. Ron Hubbard's *The Road to Freedom,* released in March 1986, comprised a Scientology musical statement. On the heels of its international release, it became a gold record.

"Thank you for listening
I write just for you."
—L. Ron Hubbard

The Way to Happiness, and his perennial advice, as contained in his song "The Good Go Free":

"Try to live a decent life
Of truth and honesty
And you will find
With a peaceful mind
The good go free."

In contrast to "The Worried Being"—drugged, harassed and obsessed with sickness—the title track is an unrestrained celebration of precisely what Scientology offers: a road of self-discovery wherein one finds,

"You are not mind or chemicals
You don't even have a form
You're in a trap of senseless lies."

Appropriately, the rhythms employ Ron's signature surge and his carefully composed melodies fully integrate with a message that effectively sums up both this album and his life:

"To you there is no limit
Knowledge is your key
Take the route of auditing
And once again be free."

The final selection, "Thank You for Listening," features a rare L. Ron Hubbard a cappella performance posthumously discovered on a demonstration cassette. Remixed and placed to music, the song becomes a fitting coda to not only the album itself, but to all that Ron had to say as Music Maker:

"Thank you for listening
I write just for you." ■

THANK YOU FOR LISTENING

Thank you for listening
I write just for you
But others hearing this may find
Things they would argue.

I do not sing what I believe
I only give them fact
If they believe quite otherwise,
It still will have impact.

For truth is truth and if they then
Decide to live with lies
That's their concern, not mine my friend,
They're free to fantasize.

The Making of
The Road to Freedom

PREMIERED AT THE INTERNATIONALLY televised celebration of Ron's birthday in March of 1986, *The Road to Freedom* became an unprecedented musical event for Scientologists world over. In addition to the release of the album itself and the debut of Ron's "Thank You for Listening," the evening featured performances by several artists heard on the tracks. What was not widely appreciated were the details of how that album came to be.

Although such an album might typically consume three or four months, work on *The Road to Freedom* factually began on 2 February 1986—or a mere five weeks before the planned release date for Ron's birthday celebration. To accomplish the feat, Scientology's Golden Era Musicians enlisted talent from the worldwide ranks of Scientology, including: Grammy award-winning arranger David Campbell, singer-songwriter David Pomeranz, acclaimed diva Julia Migenes, Chick Corea and John Travolta. Production was timetabled on a round-the-clock basis, with arrangements, recording and mixing progressing simultaneously—all of which, in no small measure, was made possible by the unique design of the L. Ron Hubbard studio. Also in play were all pertinent LRH issues: his dissection of musical form, his laws of proportionate sound, his directives on recording and mixing; and his underpinning essays on creativity as a whole. Then again—and this from Chick Corea as arranger on "Why Worship Death?"—Ron provided detailed cassettes from his mobile composing room "with very exact explanations of how he wanted it arranged."

How all came to fruition on 5 March—including final mix, pressing and jacket design—is yet another tale of LRH technology in application. Then, too, and even more to the point of music to convey key concepts of Scientology, *The Road to Freedom* was subsequently translated into French, German, Italian, Spanish, Swedish, Danish and Japanese. Finally, and just for good measure, with the international release of *The Road to Freedom*, L. Ron Hubbard's studio placed another gold record on the wall. ∎

One of two Gold Album awards for L. Ron Hubbard's *The Road to Freedom*

THE GOOD GO FREE

From L. Ron Hubbard's *The Road to Freedom* album

A concise philosophic statement of good, these lyrics convey some of the key truths contained in Scientology.

Try to live a decent life
Of truth and honesty
And you will find
With a peaceful mind
The good go free.

Chorus:
The good go free
The good go free

Be polite to your fellows
Be tolerant of the weak
And understand
That a hostile hand
Will rarely make them meek.

Avoid temptations of the flesh
For vices are a trap
And put you in
A coil of sin
Whose tentacles will enwrap.

Chorus

Fun is not found in wickedness
But in creativity
And you can court
Your favorite sport
Or pleasant industry.

Forgo all plans of vengeance
As hate was forged in Hell
And will stick you
With bitter glue
To whomever you would quell.

Don't agree with evil
Stand aside when it is planned
For an evil deed
Recoils with speed
And grips like chain and brand.

Reach outward to create your life
Produce what must be done
And be stern-willed
And very skilled
And shabby counsel shun.

Chorus

When you wake each morning
Be sure to plan your day
To only do
Good things all through
And from that do not stray.

Try to live a decent life
Of truth and honesty
And you will find
With a peaceful mind
The good go free.

Chorus

Epilogue

"The main things a musician has are what he has

created. These are the evidences as to whether or

not one is any kind of a vital force in that field."

L. RON HUBBARD

In just those terms, the vital force of L. Ron Hubbard is everywhere. It is in his delineation of musical structure and rhythm. It is in his definition of proportionate sound, his revolutionary work with the Computer Musical Instrument and his analysis of musical style. It is also, of course, in his lyrics and melodies—all of which continue to work as a vital force, sparking new ideas and directions. To cite but one example, his *Space Jazz* and *Mission Earth* albums no longer stand as the only literary soundtracks. For inspired by Ron's earlier classics, *To the Stars* and *The Ultimate Adventure*, came jazz legend Chick Corea's musical interpretations of those novels. Then, too, with dozens of compositions yet to be released—many songs and many scores—the years ahead will assuredly see much more from or inspired by L. Ron Hubbard, Music Maker.

APPENDIX

GLOSSARY

A

abiding: continuing, steadfast, unwavering. Page 31.

a cappella: (of a song) sung without instrumental accompaniment. Page 118.

acclaimed: praised publicly with great enthusiasm. Page 1.

acid rock: a form of rock music of the late 1960s and early 1970s characterized by loud electronic distortions and lyrics that refer to drug-induced experiences. Page 36.

acoustic: of the scientific study concerned with the properties of sound. Page 108.

acoustics: the qualities of a room, theater, hall, etc., that have to do with how clearly sounds can be heard or transmitted in it. Page 105.

Acropolis: the elevated, fortified section of the city of Athens, Greece. Beginning in the fifth century B.C., the Greeks built a series of structures there, including a temple dedicated to the city's patron goddess, Athena, and several theaters. Page 54.

affinity: a natural liking for or attraction to a person, thing, idea, etc. Page 24.

aficionado: a person who is very knowledgeable and enthusiastic about an activity or subject. Page 47.

aggregate, in the: as a whole; generally. Page 84.

air brakes: brakes used, especially on a motor vehicle, that are operated by *compressed air,* air that is kept in a container under pressure, often used to power machines. Page 74.

airplay: the playing of a recording over radio or TV. Page 38.

airwaves, the: radio broadcasting time, from the literal meaning of *airwaves,* the waves of energy that are used for broadcasting radio programs. Page 13.

alien: foreign in nature or character; belonging to something else. Page 2.

alongside (of): figuratively, at the same time as or in coexistence with. From the literal meaning of *alongside,* close to the side of; next to. Page 67.

Alpert, Herb: (1935–) American musician whose trumpet pieces achieved widespread popularity. As cofounder of a record company (A&M Records), he produced many hit recordings by well-known artists. Page 46.

Amazonian: having to do with the culture of peoples living in the Amazon River basin in South America. Page 2.

ambulant: characterized by moving around from place to place. Page 8.

anomalies: things that deviate from what is standard or normal; irregularities. Page 108.

apartment piano: a reference to an *upright piano,* a piano with a rectangular upright case in which the strings are mounted vertically and the keyboard is at right angles to the case. This type of piano is small enough to fit into an apartment. Page 21.

Appalachian: of or relating to the people and culture of, particularly, the central and southern parts of the *Appalachians,* a mountain system of eastern North America, nearly parallel with the Atlantic coast and extending from the province of Quebec in Canada to northern Alabama, in the southern United States. Page 26.

appointed: provided with or equipped with things that are needed. Page 109.

aptly: suitably; appropriately. Page 59.

arranging: choosing the instruments and adding chords and backup to a melody. *See also* **chord.** Page 2.

arrogantly: in a way that is *arrogant,* showing proud self-importance and contempt or disregard for others. Page 11.

Arrow Sport: a small biplane (having two sets of wings, one above the other) built during the 1920s and 1930s by the Arrow Aircraft and Motor Company of Nebraska. The Arrow Sport featured side-by-side seating in an open cockpit equipped with dual controls. It had a maximum speed of 105 miles per hour (169 kilometers per hour) and a range of 280 miles (450 kilometers). Page 44.

articulation: the clear and distinct pronunciation of words. Page 84.

Asiatic Fleet: one of the three fleets that the United States naval forces were divided into during the early and mid-twentieth century. The Asiatic Fleet was mostly in the Philippines. Page 16.

Athens: the capital and largest city of Greece, situated in the southeastern part of the country. Athens has been a center of Greek culture since the fifth century B.C. Page 53.

atmospheric: having or producing an emotional mood, tone or quality. Page 75.

audiophile: a person who is especially interested in high-fidelity sound reproduction. Page 65.

auditing: the application of Dianetics and Scientology techniques (called *processes*). Processes are directly concerned with increasing the ability of the individual to survive, with increasing his sanity or ability to reason, his physical ability and his general enjoyment of life. Also called *processing*. Page 118.

auspicious: favoring or promising success. Page 59.

Autry, Gene: (1907–1998) American musician, actor and business executive, born in Texas and known as "The Singing Cowboy." Autry started out as a singer in 1928, recorded his first hit in 1931 and shortly thereafter had his own radio show. He became a popular film star and appeared in a long series of musical westerns, usually with his horse Champion. After serving in World War II (1939–1945), he successfully returned to entertainment and in 1950 had his own television show, *The Gene Autry Show*. Page 7.

B

Bach: Johann Sebastian Bach (1685–1750), German composer of works for organ, as well as church music for smaller orchestras and voices. Page 65.

Balinese: of or having to do with *Bali,* one of the islands of Indonesia. Bali is world famous for its dances, which consist of complex dance dramas drawn from Hindu myths and based on traditions hundreds of years old. Page 40.

baling wire: a reference to wire used to tie bales together. A *bale* is a large package or bundle prepared for storage, shipping or sale, especially one tightly compressed and secured by wires, hoops, cords, etc. Page 10.

balladeer: a person who sings *ballads,* any light, simple song, especially one of sentimental or romantic character. Page 10.

band shell: an outdoor platform for concerts, having a concave, nearly hemispherical back that serves as a sounding board designed to reflect the sound toward the audience. Page 31.

baritone: a deep-sounding male voice. Page 2.

bar none: with no exceptions. *Bar* means to shut in or out with or as if with bars; exclude. Page 105.

barnstorming: in the early days of aviation, touring (the country) giving short airplane rides, exhibitions of stunt flying, etc. This term comes from the use of barns as hangars. Page 44.

barometer: something that indicates a change. Literally, a *barometer* is an instrument that measures changes in atmospheric pressure as a signal of changing weather. Page 52.

Baroque: the exuberant and ornate style of music of the seventeenth and eighteenth centuries. Page 2.

basement band: a group of amateur musicians that practices or performs in a *basement,* the part of a building that is wholly or partly below ground level. Page 10.

bass: 1. a four-string guitar, usually electric, that has the same pitch and tuning as a double bass (the largest and lowest-pitched member of the violin family, usually about 6 feet [1.8 meters] high), or the part played by it. Also called *bass guitar*. Page 33.

2. a voice, instrument or sound of the lowest range. Page 36.

3. a knob that controls the low-frequency parts of sound into or out of something. Page 51.

bassed: supported or anchored by the low sound of an instrument such as a bass guitar, played along with an instrument having a higher sound. Page 46.

beachhead: a secure initial position that has been gained and can be used for further advancement; likened to a position on an enemy shoreline captured by troops in advance of an invading force. Page 81.

beat out: defeated by a rival. Page 83.

Beethoven: Ludwig van Beethoven (1770–1827), German composer of instrumental and vocal music, considered one of the greatest musicians of all time. Page 65.

benchmark: a standard of excellence, achievement, etc., against which anything similar must be measured or judged. Page 107.

bestowed: given or presented to someone, especially as a gift. Page 42.

big band: a jazz or dance band having usually sixteen to twenty players, including sections of different instruments (for example, rhythm, brass, etc.) and performing arrangements of jazz, popular dance music, etc. Page 1.

bill: a poster or handout, especially one announcing or promoting a show, circus, etc. Page 36.

billibutugun: a musical instrument of Guam, consisting of a long stick with a string stretched between its two ends. Near the center is a resonator, such as a cocoanut, which is placed on the stomach. Page 2.

blackface: black makeup used by performers in the minstrel shows of the 1800s. Page 45.

Blackfeet: a group of Native North American peoples including the Blackfeet of Montana and several tribes now living in Canada. This group controlled areas that were fought over by fur traders in the 1800s. Page 41.

black tie, in: wearing a formal style in men's dress that includes a black bow tie and a tuxedo. Page 24.

blues: a form of music expressing despair, which comes from a type of tribal chant in Africa and was imported into the cane and cotton fields as a worker's chant alongside of spirituals. This musical form then reached New Orleans and went up the Mississippi and became the basis of what was called *blues*. It ceased to be mainly choral and became a solo song sung by a person often called a *blues singer*. Page 8.

bones: a reference to necklaces or other kinds of jewelry made from bones. Page 40.

bongo(s): a pair of small, high-pitched drums, one smaller and higher-pitched than the other. Bongo drums are usually held between the knees and played with the fingers or the entire hand. Page 23.

borne out: supported, backed up or confirmed. Page 36.

Brahms: Johannes Brahms (1833–1897), German composer and one of the major composers of the nineteenth century. Page 65.

brand: 1. a lasting impression made on somebody or something. Page 86.
2. literally, a mark formerly put on criminals with a hot iron; hence, any means that indicates or points out conduct that is bad, disgraceful, criminal or the like. Page 123.

brink, at the: at a crucial or critical point, especially of a situation or state beyond which success or catastrophe occurs. Literally, the very edge of a steep place, such as the *brink* of a cliff. Page 73.

British Columbian: of or having to do with British Columbia, a province in western Canada on the Pacific coast. Page 12.

C

Cádiz: a seaport in southwestern Spain, on a bay of the Atlantic. Page 28.

calypso: a musical style of West Indian origin, influenced by jazz, usually having improvised lyrics reflecting current interests. Page 41.

Campbell, Jr., John W.: (1910–1971) American editor and writer who began writing science fiction while at college. In 1937 Campbell was appointed editor of the magazine *Astounding Stories,* later titled *Astounding Science Fiction* and then *Analog.* Under his editorship *Astounding* became a major influence in the development of science fiction and published stories by some of the most important writers of that time. Page 16.

campfire: a fire usually built outdoors (as in a camp or on a picnic) for cooking, heat or light; especially, such a fire designed to serve as the central point of a social gathering. Page 7.

cane and cotton fields: fields of sugar cane and cotton, primary agricultural products of the southern part of the US during the 1800s. Page 67.

cannery fleet: a group of fishing vessels that supply fish to a *cannery,* a factory for putting fish into cans. Canneries have existed in ports such as Ketchikan since the late 1800s, mainly handling the salmon that are fished in the area. Page 14.

canter: the way a horse moves when it is traveling at a smooth, easy, fast pace. Page 39.

Carabobo: a state in the northern part of *Venezuela,* a country in northeastern South America, on the Caribbean Sea and the Atlantic Ocean. Page 13.

Caribbean: the islands and countries of the Caribbean Sea collectively. The Caribbean Sea is a part of the Atlantic Ocean bounded by Central America, the West Indies and South America. Page 17.

carpenter's saw: also *musical saw,* a handsaw made to produce melody by bending the blade with varying tension while striking or rubbing it with a small hammer or a violin bow. Page 11.

castanets: a small percussion instrument consisting of two cup-shaped wooden disks that are strung together. The pair of disks are held in the hand and are clicked together, producing a rhythmic accompaniment, especially by Spanish dancers. Page 27.

Chamorro: the native peoples of Guam and the Mariana Islands, in the western Pacific Ocean. Guam is the largest and southernmost of the *Mariana Islands,* a group of fifteen small islands in the Pacific, east of the Philippines and China. Page 9.

chantey: a sailor's song, especially one sung in rhythm to work. Page 35.

charts: a list of the musical recordings that have sold the most copies during a specific period. Page 82.

Chinese zither: also called *qin,* an ancient Chinese musical instrument. The qin consists of a flat wooden soundbox across which are seven strings that are plucked by the performer. Page 10.

Chopin: Frédéric Chopin (1810–1849), Polish composer and pianist ranked as one of the masters of piano composition. Page 65.

Choralizer: a unique device that gives a choruslike effect to music sounds, hence its name. The Choralizer consists of two microphones in a small chamber that also has a loudspeaker. Sounds from the loudspeaker reflect off the walls of the chamber and are captured by the microphones, which spin while moving up and down. Subtle pitch variations as the microphones approach and recede from the walls of the chamber produce a variety of tones, creating a rich sound that blends what seems to be many instruments or voices. *See also* **Doppler effect.** Page 109.

chord: a combination of three or more notes sounding at the same time. A *minor chord* is one using notes from a minor scale and thus having a moody or touching quality. A *major chord* is one using notes from a major scale and thus having a bright or joyous sound. *See also* **minors.** Page 81.

chord progression: in music, a movement from one chord (three or more notes sounding at the same time) to another; a succession of chords or tones. Page 85.

choreograph(ing): arrange the movements of a dance. Page 33.

choreography: the art and skill of arranging the movements of a dance. Page 23.

coda: a concluding section or part serving as a summation of preceding themes, motifs, etc., as in a work of literature or drama; anything that serves as a concluding part; in music specifically, a more or less independent passage at the end of a composition, introduced to bring it to a satisfactory close. Page 118.

coil: figuratively, something that binds, restricts or entangles. From the literal meaning of *coil*, a length of something, such as rope, that is arranged into a series of circles, one above the other. Page 123.

collective: of or characteristic of a group of individuals taken together. Page 37.

Coltrane, John: (1926–1967) American saxophone player and composer whose performances have been recognized as among the most influential in jazz music. Page 65.

combo: a small jazz or dance band having usually from three to six players. Page 1.

concert grand: also called *concert grand piano*. A *grand piano* is a large, full-toned, wing-shaped piano, supported by three legs, in which the body and strings are arranged horizontally. A *concert grand* is the largest size of grand piano, between 9 to 12 feet (2.74 to 3.66 meters) long, and is designed for use in a concert hall. Page 24.

conga(s): a tall, narrow drum that is played with both hands, used in Latin American and African music. Page 23.

contention: a statement or point that one argues for as true. Page 69.

control room: a room from which a recording session is controlled. It contains the equipment and instruments used to record sound. Page 105.

convex: curving outward like the surface of a sphere. Page 108.

counted: considered or regarded. Page 1.

counter-rhythm: a second rhythm underlying the drum rhythm, usually at lower pitch than the drums. This counter-rhythm would surge exactly in the same way as the rest of the beat. Page 61.

course(s): a set of strings of the same tone placed beside one another. The player can then strike one or more strings at a time, according to the strength of sound desired. Page 13.

court: 1. attempt to win the support or favor of. Also, risk incurring (misfortune) because of the way one behaves. Page 69.
2. show that one is interested in something or wants to become involved in something. Page 123.

Crosby, Bing: (1903–1977) popular American singer and motion picture star. His more than one thousand records have sold over three hundred million copies and he also appeared in more than fifty films. Page 16.

cuatro: a small guitar, typically with four single or paired strings, used in Latin American and Caribbean folk music. The Spanish word *cuatro* means four. Page 13.

Curaçao: an island in the southern Caribbean Sea, lying off the coast of Venezuela. The island, an autonomous country within the Kingdom of the Netherlands, is a popular tourist destination. Page 42.

cut: a penetrating quality in a musical instrument or voice; a quality that makes a sound stand out, sometimes harshly. Page 46.

cutting-edge: in the most advanced or innovative position. Page 1.

Davis, Miles: (1926–1991) American trumpet player and bandleader, one of the most innovative and influential figures in the history of jazz. Page 65.

dead on: exactly right; accurate. Page 33.

death-dealing: that brings death. Page 62.

decibel: a unit of sound measurement. Decibels show exact quantities of loudness. Page 84.

de rigueur: strictly required, as by current usage. Page 60.

Dianetics: Dianetics is a forerunner and substudy of Scientology. Dianetics means "through the mind" or "through the soul" (from Greek *dia,* through, and *nous,* mind or soul). It is a system of coordinated axioms which resolve problems concerning human behavior and psychosomatic illnesses. It combines a workable technique and a thoroughly validated method for increasing sanity, by erasing unwanted sensations and unpleasant emotions. Page 1.

dictum: a short statement that expresses a general truth or principle. Page 33.

didgeridoo: an Australian aboriginal musical instrument consisting of a long thick wooden pipe that the player blows into, creating a deep, reverberating humming sound. Page 26.

dirty: characterized by a raw, harsh tonal quality; not melodious. Page 74.

dissect(ed): examine minutely, part by part; analyze. Page 2.

dissection: the action or an instance of examining something minutely, part by part; analysis. Page 2.

diva: a distinguished female singer. Page 121.

dockage: the berthing of a ship at a *dock,* a platform built out into the sea, a river, etc., where boats can be tied and where people and goods can be brought aboard or taken off. Page 31.

doom: dreadful fate, especially death or utter ruin. Page 77.

Doppler effect: the apparent change in pitch when a source of sound is moving in relationship to an observer. For example, the pitch of a siren seems higher when a police car or fire engine approaches an observer and lower after it passes and begins to move away. In fact, the actual pitch of the siren does not change. (Named for Christian Doppler [1803–1853], Austrian mathematician and physicist, who first explained the phenomenon.) Page 109.

Dover shore: an area on Vancouver Island, British Columbia, roughly 500 miles (800 kilometers) south of Ketchikan, Alaska. Page 14.

dovetails: joins or fits together with something else harmoniously. Page 111.

downbeats: *beat* refers to a regular emphasis or pulse of sound. For example, a common beat for rock music consists of a repeating pattern of four beats at regular intervals. In this instance, each of these four beats is a downbeat. If counted out loud, one would hear "ONE and TWO and THREE and FOUR," the four numbers being the *downbeats,* or *strong* beats. The "and" between each number would be an *upbeat,* or *weak* beat. Page 22.

drone: a pilotless aircraft, usually one whose flight is controlled by a computer, signals from a radio or the like. Page 62.

drum fills: fast drum notes that break the normal drum rhythm. They are used to "fill" a pause in a song or to introduce or emphasize transitions between two separate musical parts. Page 36.

drum kit: a set of drums, cymbals and other percussion instruments played by one person. Also called *drum set.* Page 74.

dry rot: a state of hidden or unsuspected moral or social decay, from the literal meaning of a type of decay in wood that causes it to become brittle and crumble into powder. Page 55.

dulcimer, Appalachian: a stringed musical instrument consisting of a flat wooden box with metal strings running the length of the instrument. The performer lays the dulcimer flat (in his lap, on a table, etc.) and plays the strings, usually with a small stick or the like. *See also* **Appalachian.** Page 26.

Earth Day: a worldwide observance held on April 22 each year. It began in 1970 to increase public awareness of environmental problems. Page 76.

ebbing: moving away from the land; receding. Page 14.

echo: repeat or imitate words or ideas (of a person). Page 69.

edge: force or effectiveness. Page 12.

Ellington, Duke: Edward Kennedy Ellington (1899–1974), American jazz composer, orchestrator, bandleader and pianist, considered the greatest composer in the history of jazz music with some two thousand works that include not only jazz, but also musical comedy, ballet and opera. Page 65.

Emotional Tone Scale: a scale that shows the successive emotional tones a person can experience. By *tone* is meant the momentary or continuing emotional state of a person. Emotions such as fear, anger, grief, enthusiasm and others which people experience are shown on this graduated scale. A Tone Scale tells you how people behave. If people are at a certain level on the Tone Scale, then they behave in a certain way and you can predict how they will behave. Page 36.

engender: bring into existence; produce. Page 79.

engineer, line: also called *recording engineer,* the person responsible for properly recording a program, such as with one or more voices or instruments, using the equipment that makes up the recording line, usually including such things as microphones, recorders and other types of equipment. Page 110.

engineer, recording: also called *line engineer. See also* **engineer, line.** Page 49.

en masse: all together as a whole; in a mass. Page 33.

ensemble: a group of dancers, musicians, etc., that perform together. Page 38.

enwrap: wrap or closely surround with. Page 123.

ethnological: of or having to do with *ethnology,* the science that analyzes cultures, especially in regard to their historical development and the similarities and dissimilarities between them. Page 12.

Evans, Bill: William John Evans (1929–1980), renowned jazz pianist whose remarkable piano performances became the single most influential style through the mid and late 1900s. Page 65.

evocative: tending to call up or produce a vivid impression of reality through artistry and imagination. Page 2.

exalted: grand or noble in character. Page 61.

expressly: for the particular or specific purpose; specially. Page 106.

eye to, with an: with a view to; with the object or intention of. Page 36.

Ff

---

far-flung: extended far or to a great distance; remote. Page 9.

fathom: understand (something) after much thought. Page 1.

fickle: unpredictable; likely to change without warning. Page 83.

fiddle: a stringed musical instrument, the violin. Violins are often called *fiddles* in folk music or country music. Page 7.

fidelity: the degree of accuracy with which sound or images are recorded or reproduced. Page 105.

fills, drum: fast drum notes that break the normal drum rhythm. They are used to "fill" a pause in a song or to introduce or emphasize transitions between two separate musical parts. Page 36.

fisherfolk: people who catch fish for a living. Page 13.

fission: the splitting of the central part of an atom (nucleus) into fragments. The pieces of the nucleus then strike other nuclei (centers of atoms) and cause them to fission (split), thus creating a chain reaction, which is accompanied by a significant release of energy. Page 77.

Fitzgerald, Ella: (1917–1996) celebrated American jazz singer who recorded with the greats of jazz performance. In a career spanning almost sixty years, she won numerous awards, including fourteen Grammy awards. Page 65.

flamenco: the Spanish gypsy style of dance (characterized by stamping, clapping, etc.) or music (typically very emotional and mournful). Page 38.

Ford Foundation: a privately owned institution founded in 1936 by contributions from American automobile manufacturers Henry Ford (1863–1947) and his son Edsel Ford (1893–1943). The foundation issues grants for a variety of projects, including those in the areas of education and culture. Page 46.

forgo: give up. Page 123.

forged: created; formed. Page 123.

forty-niner: characteristic of those persons, especially prospectors, who went to California in the 1849 gold rush. Page 7.

Foster, Stephen: Stephen Collins Foster (1826–1864), American composer of many widely popular songs, such as "Oh, Susanna" (1848). He wrote more than two hundred songs, including a number that were performed in the minstrel shows of the nineteenth century. Page 45.

friend: a person who gives assistance; patron; supporter (as in *Friends of the United Nations*). Page 76.

Funchal: the seaport capital of the *Madeira Islands,* a group of eight islands off the northwest coast of Africa, a part of Portugal. Page 38.

G

---

gait: a way of walking, running or moving along on foot. Page 39.

galvanizing: stimulating into sudden activity; startling. Page 37.

gamelan gongs: a *gamelan* is an Indonesian musical ensemble consisting of wind, string and percussion instruments, including flute, lute, drums, bamboo xylophones and gongs. The gongs belonging to this ensemble are often termed *pot gongs*. Made of bronze, these gongs have been manufactured in Indonesia for at least one thousand years. Page 10.

garage band: a group of amateur musicians that practices or performs in a *garage,* a building attached to a house where a car can be stored. Page 31.

garb: a style of clothing, especially distinctive or official. Page 40.

genre(s): a category of artistic composition, as in music or literature, marked by a distinctive style, form or content. Page 59.

genus: origin. From the Latin *genus,* meaning origin, birth or race. Page 53.

George Washington University: a private university, founded in 1821, in the city of Washington, DC. Named after the first president of the United States, George Washington (1732–1799), it maintains various schools of education, including the School of Engineering and Applied Science and the Columbian College of Arts and Sciences. The university has a long history of supporting research in physics and other technical fields. Page 11.

Gershwin: George Gershwin (1898–1937), American composer whose immensely popular songs and orchestral and piano works, such as *Rhapsody in Blue* (1924), blend classical music styles with the rhythms of popular music and jazz. Page 33.

Godfrey, Arthur: (1903–1983) an American radio and television broadcaster and entertainer. Page 2.

Golden Age of Greece: a *Golden Age* is the most flourishing period in the history of something; the time of highest achievement or greatest development. The Greek civilization that thrived around the Mediterranean Sea from circa 3000 B.C. to the first century B.C. is noted for its Golden Age (480 to 323 B.C.), when the ancient Greeks reached their highest prosperity and produced their highest cultural accomplishments in art, architecture, drama, philosophy and government. Page 54.

Graham, Martha: (1893–1991) American choreographer, dancer and teacher, the most influential figure in American modern dance for more than fifty years. With dance pieces based on compositions by the foremost composers, she choreographed over 150 works during her career. Page 52.

Gran Baile de Gala: *de gala* means full dress. The *Gran Baile de Gala* is a large annual ball or dance held, with people attending in their finery. Page 42.

Great Falls: a city in central Montana, a state in the northwestern United States bordering on Canada. Page 7.

gregarious: marked by friendliness; social. Page 7.

grip on: a proper understanding or control of something. Page 67.

Guam: a territory of the United States, the largest of the *Mariana Islands,* a group of fifteen small islands in the Pacific, east of the Philippines and China. Page 9.

Guamanian: of or relating to Guam. *See also* **Guam.** Page 2.

H

---

harness: gain control of something and use it for some purpose. Page 1.

haunts: places frequently visited. Page 35.

heed: give careful attention to. Page 69.

heels of, on the: closely following; just after. Page 117.

Helena: city and capital of Montana, a state in the northwestern United States bordering on Canada. Page 7.

Herman, Woody: (1913–1987) American jazz saxophonist, clarinetist and bandleader who for more than fifty years led one of the most consistently popular big bands in jazz. Page 1.

heyday: the stage or period of greatest vigor, strength, success, etc. Page 45.

high-end: high-quality; top-of-the-line; sophisticated. Page 65.

high-fidelity: concerned with or capable of extremely high-quality sound reproduction with minimal distortion and where the sound produced bears as close a resemblance as possible to the original. *Fidelity* means the degree of accuracy with which sound or images are recorded or reproduced. Page 109.

hillbilly: of or characteristic of the culture existing in areas such as the mountains of the southern United States. Page 46.

hoedown: a community dancing party featuring folk and square dances, accompanied by hillbilly tunes played on the fiddle. Page 7.

hoist bucket: a bucket that is *hoisted,* raised or lifted by some mechanical means, to bring something up to a higher level. Page 60.

hold your hat(s): an expression used as a warning to tell a person or a group of people to be prepared for a shock, surprise or very intense series of events, as if enough to make one's hat fly off. Page 83.

Holiday, Billie: stage name of Eleanora Fagan (1915–1959), one of the greatest jazz-blues singers of all time. Page 65.

honky-tonk: a type of country music from the 1940s and 1950s with a strong beat. Honky-tonk makes use of a piano whose strings have been muffled and given a characteristic tinny sound. Page 59.

Hydrographic Office: a section of the Department of the Navy charged with making hydrographic surveys and publishing charts and other information for naval and commercial vessels, information key to national defense. *Hydrographic* means of or relating to the scientific charting, description and analysis of the physical conditions, boundaries and flow of oceans, lakes, rivers, etc. Page 12.

I

Iberian: relating to or typical of the people or culture of the Iberian peninsula in southwestern Europe, which consists primarily of the countries of Spain and Portugal. Page 37.

imprint, bear (one's): receive and hold a lasting effect or characteristic result or influence. Page 36.

impromptu: made or done on the spur of the moment; hastily made for the occasion. Page 7.

inarguable: not open to debate, challenge or doubt. Page 37.

incisive: sharp, keen, penetrating; of speech or writing, seeming to penetrate directly to the heart of the matter, resulting in a clear and definite statement. Page 44.

indigenous: originating in and characteristic of a particular region or country; native. Page 7.

industry: close, steady work or involvement in some activity, resulting in worthwhile production. Page 123.

inflection, vocal: change or variation of pitch (high and low) or loudness of the voice. Page 24.

ins and outs: detailed facts and points (about something). Page 80.

instrumentation: 1. composition or arrangement of music for performance, in which a combination of musical instruments is specified. Page 1.

2. the type of instruments used in a musical piece. Page 10.

intrinsic(ally): belonging to something as one of the basic and essential elements that make it what it is. Page 21.

irradiate: expose or overexpose to radiation. Page 77.

J

---

jackboots: boots of sturdy leather reaching up to, or over, the knee, worn especially by soldiers. Page 62.

jam session(s): a meeting of a group of musicians, especially jazz musicians, usually to play for their own enjoyment. Page 12.

Javanese: of or pertaining to the island of *Java,* the main island of Indonesia. Page 10.

Javanese temple gongs: same as *gamelan gongs.* A *gamelan* is an Indonesian musical ensemble consisting of wind, string and percussion instruments, including flute, lute, drums, bamboo xylophones and gongs. The gongs belonging to this ensemble are often termed *pot gongs.* Made of bronze, these gongs have been manufactured in Indonesia for at least one thousand years. Page 65.

K

Ketchikan: a seaport in southeastern Alaska, one of the chief ports on Alaska's Pacific coast. Ketchikan is a transportation and communications center. Page 13.

KGBU: the group of letters (termed *call letters*) that identify a radio transmitting station, in this case the public radio station located in Ketchikan, Alaska. Radio KGBU operated from the late 1920s until the early 1940s. It was the second radio station in Alaska. Page 13.

koto: a Japanese musical instrument with a rectangular body and from seven to thirteen waxed silk strings. Page 10.

L

lamé: an ornamental fabric in which metallic threads, as of gold or silver, are woven with silk, wool, rayon or cotton. Page 40.

lament(s): a formal expression of sorrow or mourning, especially in verse or in song. Page 7.

late as it thinks, isn't as: not so far advanced into a bad state as had been thought and therefore capable of being mended or put right. Page 55.

launch: start (a person) on a course, career, etc. Page 2.

laying down: recording instruments, percussion, voices, etc., on their own separate tracks. Page 75.

Lexan (panels): large sheets of Lexan (a brand of tough, clear plastic) used to reflect sound for recording. An instrument or vocal performer sends out sounds in many directions, but not all these sounds arrive at the microphone. Lexan panels are curved in a mathematically precise way to redirect the sounds without changing or distorting them, thus enabling the microphone to capture all the rich and varied tones of instrument and voice. Page 108.

lilting: characterized by a gentle rhythm in a tune. Page 7.

limiter: a piece of electronic equipment that limits the intensity or loudness of a sound. Page 84.

Lisbon: a seaport in and the capital of Portugal, in the southwestern part of the country. Page 38.

literary soundtrack: a sound accompaniment (soundtrack) for a book; music written to accompany a book. Page 1.

living up to their name: matching by means of action what the name says, here referring to the word "star" in the name *Apollo Stars,* meaning that they became stars in terms of popularity. Page 38.

looms: comes into view, shows up, as if in a magnified, almost threatening manner. Page 77.

lore: acquired knowledge or wisdom on a particular subject, for example, local traditions, handed down by word of mouth and usually in the form of stories or historical anecdotes. Page 35.

lose its way in the woods: (also *lose course*) go off in the wrong direction, as by changing successful patterns; go down to a lower level. Page 54.

low-caste: a *caste* is any class or group of society sharing common cultural features. *Low* means ranked near the beginning or bottom on some scale of measurement. Therefore *low-caste* is any class or group of society considered to be lesser in some way to other classes or groups of society. Page 11.

luminaries: persons who inspire or influence others. Page 117.

Madeira: the chief island of the *Madeira Islands,* a group of eight islands off the northwest coast of Africa, a part of Portugal. Page 31.

madrigal: a song with parts for several voices singing without accompaniment, popular from the fifteenth through the seventeenth centuries. Page 65.

mail buoy: a *buoy* is an anchored float serving as a navigation mark, to show hazards or for mooring. A "mail buoy" is a prank used on naval ships in which new recruits are told to stand watch at the bow of the ship for a buoy that passing ships supposedly attach mail to. Used humorously as the name of LRH's radio program in Ketchikan, Alaska, a program in which listeners' questions were taken up and answered. Page 13.

major chord: in music, a chord (a combination of three or more notes sounding at the same time) that is associated with specific emotional qualities, usually brightness and joy, as opposed to a minor chord, which is generally considered more moody or touching. *See also* **minors.** Page 81.

mandolin: a stringed musical instrument with a pear-shaped body and four or more pairs of strings. Page 39.

maracas: a percussion instrument, usually shaken in pairs as an accompaniment to Latin American music and consisting of a hollow rattle filled with small pebbles or beans. Page 26.

Marineros: one of several musical groups formed by LRH to provide entertainment at the ports that his research vessel *Apollo* would regularly visit. Playing a style of pop called *Progressiva,* the Marineros (taken from the Spanish word meaning *sailor*) delighted audiences at their many venues. *See also* **Progressiva.** Page 38.

Martinique: an island in the West Indies (a group of islands in the Atlantic between North and South America). It was colonized by French settlers after 1635. Page 81.

master mariner: a *master* is the captain of a *merchant vessel,* any ship employed in commerce. A *mariner* is a sailor or navigator who sails or navigates vessels at sea. Licensed to take command of a merchant vessel, *master mariners* are those individuals with demonstrated competence in such skills as emergency and safety operation, navigation, meteorology (the science of the atmosphere, weather and weather forecasting), radar, radio communication, ship handling, cargo operations and equipment, and maritime law. Page 13.

measure: a small portion of the overall piece of music, each portion having so many beats (such as four). Page 22.

measure, for good: as a bonus or something extra. Page 2.

mellow: (of sound) soft, not strong or unpleasant. Page 16.

met count: the number of pulses or beats per minute as produced by a *metronome,* a device that produces a regular repeated sound (tick), like a clock, used by musicians to help them keep a rhythmic time in playing their music. The device can be set to produce faster or slower ticks. Page 67.

meter: rhythm in verse; measured, patterned arrangement of syllables, primarily according to stress or length. Page 73.

meter volume: the level of volume of a piece as registered on a meter, specifically, on a *volume meter,* a meter used with sound-reproducing or recording equipment that measures loudness. Page 51.

metronome: a device that produces a regular repeated sound (tick), like a clock, used by musicians to help them keep a rhythmic time in playing their music. The device can be set to produce faster or slower ticks. Page 33.

Middle West: the northern region of the central United States east of the Rocky Mountains. The area is known for its rich farmlands. Page 46.

mike: to place and handle microphones in order to obtain the best quality sound with them. Page 51.

military drum: a type of drum often used in military bands. Traditionally, such drums have a rope running diagonally from the top of the drum to the bottom, forming a pattern of slanted lines around the outside of the drum. This rope is tightened (or loosened), affecting the sound of the drum. Page 46.

Miller, Glenn: Alton Glenn Miller (1904–1944), American musician and bandleader, one of the most popular performing artists of the late 1930s and early 1940s. Miller's distinctive style of band music has remained popular, with rereleases of his songs over the years. Page 48.

minors: a reference to one of the two main scales in music (major and minor) that provides a distinct emotional quality to a musical piece. A *scale* is a series of musical notes arranged sequentially in ascending or descending order of pitch, such as those represented on a piano keyboard. Composers use different scales to convey mood or emotion in a melody. A minor scale, due to its pattern of notes, is generally considered more moody or touching as contrasted with a major scale, which is usually associated with brightness or joy. *See also* **major chord.** Page 81.

minstrel show: American theatrical entertainment popular during the 1800s, consisting of songs and dances accompanied by banjo, violin and tambourine, interspersed with jokes and comic skits. Page 10.

Mississippi (River) steamboat: a reference to a type of steam-driven large boat. The Mississippi River is the largest river in North America, flowing south from Minnesota, in the north central US, down to the Gulf of Mexico. During the 1800s, travel on steamboats became extremely popular with the influx of new settlers. Page 10.

mix: putting several tracks onto the two stereo or four quad tracks of the final product. It is done through a mixing board. *See also* **quad.** Page 51.

Mongolia: a nation in eastern Asia, bordered on the north by Russia and on the east, south and west by China. Page 65.

Motown: a style of music of the 1960s and 1970s, consisting of elements of pop, soul and gospel. The name comes from its early popularity in Detroit, Michigan (a state in the north central United States). It is a shortening of *Motor Town,* a nickname for Detroit, from the city's association with the auto industry. Page 23.

mouth organ: a *harmonica,* a musical instrument consisting of a small narrow metal case containing a set of metal reeds (thin pieces fitted inside that vibrate to produce sound) connected to a row of holes over which the player places the mouth and exhales and inhales to produce tones. Page 7.

Mozart: Wolfgang Amadeus Mozart (1756–1791), Austrian composer of opera, orchestral and vocal music. Page 65.

musicianship: knowledge, skill in playing or performing music. Page 73.

N

namesake: person having the same name as another. Page 10.

Nazareth, Pennsylvania: a city in the United States known for being the global headquarters for C. F. Martin & Company, the manufacturer of Martin guitars. Page 13.

net effect: final result that comes about after all individual elements have been included. Page 37.

note time value: in music, the duration of a note. Page 67.

nucleus: a central part about which other parts are grouped or gathered; core. Page 38.

O

octave, thirteen-note: in music, an *octave* is the span between any note and a note eight steps higher (from *octo,* eight). These eight steps are often referred to as *do, re, mi, fa, sol, la, ti, do*. The octave can also be broken down into smaller steps, so that thirteen such steps are heard from the lower note to the higher note. Page 62.

"Oh, Susanna": a song written in 1848 by American composer Stephen Collins Foster (1826–1864). An exuberant, carefree song, "Oh, Susanna" became a favorite of the *forty-niners,* those who went to California during the gold rush of 1849. Page 8.

Orient: the countries of eastern Asia, especially China, Japan and their neighbors. Page 2.

oscilloscope: an electronic instrument that displays changing electrical signals. The signals appear as wavy lines or in other patterns on a screen. Page 111.

Ozarked: of or having to do with the *Ozarks,* a mountainous region of the south central US with a strong tradition of country western music. Page 39.

P

pace, set the: establish a standard that others have to keep up with. Page 86.

Palm Springs: a resort and residential city in Southern California, USA. Page 47.

palomino: a horse with a golden coat, a white mane and tail and, often, white markings on the face and legs. Page 60.

Panhandle: part of the state of Alaska that extends along the Pacific coast, south from the main part of the state. A *panhandle* is a narrow section of land shaped like the handle of a cooking pan, that extends away from the body of the state it belongs to. Page 12.

parchments: stiff, strong papers that are smooth or textured, used for special documents, letters or artwork. Page 69.

par excellence: in the greatest degree of excellence; beyond comparison. Page 110.

park walk: a walking pace for a horse that is performed in a flashy, high-stepping fashion. The term *park* or *park action* refers to a gait developed to show off the skill of both the horse and the rider, as for riding in city parks on Sundays. Page 39.

penny arcade: an amusement center or area that contains coin-operated entertainment devices, originally operated for a penny a play. Page 8.

percussion: *percussion* means intensity plus hit or impact. It is a study of the factors of entrance (start) and decay (decrease in intensity or volume) of a note in terms of *duration,* the time during which something continues. Page 37.

Persian romance: a story from *Persia,* the ancient empire of central Asia, which is present-day Iran. Persian literature has traditionally been dominated by poetry, with poems being included within almost every type of writing, including *romances,* stories describing exciting and heroic deeds and adventures, usually in a historical or imaginary setting. Page 73.

philosophic: concerned with the study of the truths or principles underlying all knowledge, being (reality) or conduct. From Greek *philos,* "loving" and *sophia,* "learning." Page 22.

physiological: relating to the body and how it is observed to be functioning. From the science of *physiology,* which studies the functions and activities of living organisms and their parts, including all physical and chemical processes. Page 84.

pix: plural of *pic,* a slang shortening of *picture,* meaning a movie. Page 79.

plumb: examine closely in order to discover or understand, as if having gone all the way through something to the bottom of it, likened to reaching the bottom with a *plumb,* a small mass of lead or other heavy material suspended by a line and used to measure the depth of water. Page 52.

Port Orchard: a resort and fishing community located in western Washington State on *Puget Sound,* a long, narrow bay of the Pacific Ocean on the northwestern coast of the United States. Page 12.

port-side: the area beside or near a port. Page 31.

port(s) of call: a harbor town or city where ships can visit during the course of a voyage. Page 37.

posthumously: in a manner that is *posthumous,* occurring after the author's lifetime. Page 118.

posting: an appointment to a job, especially one abroad or in the armed forces. Page 9.

presciently: with a knowledge of things before they exist or happen. Page 60.

press box: a section of a sports stadium reserved for media to report about events occurring there. Newspaper writers and television and radio announcers report from the press box. Page 39.

primal: being first, original. Page 75.

Progressiva: far-out pop music that went beyond the standard songs of rock or popular music. Progressiva had a good, fast rhythm and was especially popular from the late 1960s to the mid-1970s. Page 38.

pursuit: any occupation, pastime or the like, in which a person is engaged regularly or customarily. Page 2.

puts over: causes to be understood or accepted. Page 16.

quad: short for *quadraphonic* sound, high-fidelity sound reproduction involving signals transmitted through four channels. Page 51.

quarter note: in musical notation, a note with one-fourth the time value of a whole note. Page 85.

quell: suppress; put an end to. Page 123.

quest: a search or pursuit made in order to find or obtain something. Page 77.

R

rallying cry: a phrase expressing the aims or nature of an enterprise, organization, etc.; a motto. Page 76.

rapport: relationship, especially one of mutual trust or affinity. An audience in rapport is different than an audience of spectators. An audience in rapport participates in small or large ways with the performer or the artist or work of art, often by vocal or body motion. Page 22.

real time: the actual time during which something happens. Page 110.

recoils: (of an action) comes back or reacts with an unfavorable consequence on (the originator). Page 123.

reel: also *Virginia reel,* an American country dance in which the partners start by facing each other in two lines. Page 7.

reggae: a style of rhythmic Jamaican popular music blending blues, calypso and rock and roll. Page 41.

rejoice: to make joyful. Page 1.

Renaissance: of the period in European history from the early 1300s to the 1600s, marked by a revival of art, literature and learning. From the Latin *re,* again, and *nasci,* to be born. Page 65.

repertoire: a stock of musical or dramatic material that is known and can be performed by a musician, musical group, actor, etc.; material available for performance. Page 16.

replete: abundantly supplied or provided; filled. Page 38.

requiem: a solemn chant, song, poem or the like, as for the dead. Page 117.

reverberation: sound that echoes back and forth. Page 109.

revving: (of an engine, as of an automobile, motorcycle or the like) increasing its speed, especially while the vehicle is being held stationary. *Rev* is short for *revolution,* from the turning or spinning of the main shaft of the engine. Page 60.

rhumba: a dance, Cuban in origin and complex in rhythm. The rhumba emphasizes a swaying hip motion that is achieved by taking small steps with the knees relaxed. Page 17.

Rich, Buddy: (1917–1987) American jazz drummer and bandleader billed as "the world's greatest drummer." Known for his brilliant technique, power and speed, he played with several big bands, started several short-lived bands of his own and often performed solo. Page 1.

riff: a musical phrase or series of notes, often constantly repeated. Page 36.

rightist regime: a conservative government (regime) exercising rigid controls. Page 31.

road, took to the: set out or began traveling. Page 94.

rockabilly: an early form of rock and roll with a strong country music influence. Page 36.

Rogers, Roy: (born Leonard Slye, 1911–1998) American actor and singer known as the "King of the Cowboys." In 1938 he changed his name to Roy Rogers and performed his first starring role in a motion picture titled *Under the Western Stars*. Usually astride his faithful horse Trigger, Rogers appeared in about ninety westerns, continuing into the early 1950s. Page 7.

rooting down: placing something firmly, likened to having roots in the ground. Page 75.

rugged degrade, running a: creating conditions or situations that are rough or difficult and that are becoming worse. Page 55.

rug was already coming out from underneath: (one's) activities, plans and expectations were beginning to fail (from the expression *pull the rug out from underneath someone*). Page 54.

rushed the stage: (of an audience) moved forward quickly onto the stage during or after a performance. Page 37.

S
_____

Saint Hill Hubbard College: the Hubbard College of Scientology, located at Saint Hill Manor in East Grinstead, Sussex, in southern England, in the mid-1960s. It had the purpose of training the best auditors in the world. An auditor is a Dianetics or Scientology practitioner. The word *auditor* means one who listens; a listener. Page 12.

Saint Hill Manor: a manor (a large house and its land) located in East Grinstead, Sussex, in southern England. Saint Hill Manor was the residence of L. Ron Hubbard as well as the international communications and training center of Scientology from the late 1950s through the mid-1960s. Page 21.

Santa Cruz de Tenerife: the chief city on *Tenerife,* the largest island of the Canary Islands, off the northwest coast of Africa. Page 12.

satire: a literary work in which vices, follies, stupidities, abuses, etc., are held up to ridicule and contempt. Page 73.

savage breast, the: the primitive emotions in a person, from the figurative idea that the breast (the front part of a person's chest) is the center of emotions. In reference to the line "Music has charms to soothe the savage breast," by English playwright and poet William Congreve (1670–1729). Page 37.

saw, carpenter's: also *musical saw,* a handsaw made to produce melody by bending the blade with varying tension while striking or rubbing it with a small hammer or a violin bow. Page 11.

sawing: playing a stringed instrument (such as a fiddle) with a bow. This is so called as the motion of the bow is similar to the back-and-forth motion used in sawing a piece of wood. Page 7.

sax: an informal name for a *saxophone,* a metal wind instrument used especially in jazz and dance music. Page 10.

scan, in: within view. Page 14.

schooner: a sailing ship with sails set lengthwise (fore and aft) and having from two to as many as seven masts. Page 35.

Scientology: Scientology is the study and handling of the spirit in relationship to itself, universes and other life. The term Scientology is taken from the Latin *scio,* which means "knowing in the fullest sense of the word," and the Greek word *logos,* meaning "study of." In itself the word means literally "knowing how to know." Page 1.

sea dog: a sailor, especially an old or experienced one. Page 35.

seafaring: of or engaged in life at sea, such as by being a sailor. Page 35.

Secret of Treasure Island, The: the series of films produced by Columbia Pictures, drawn from the L. Ron Hubbard novel *Murder at Pirate Castle.* LRH's screenplays for the serial, written during 1937, became a box office success. Page 35.

Senegal: a country in western Africa on the Atlantic Ocean. Formerly a French colony, Senegal became independent in 1960. Page 65.

Setúbal: a seaport in southwestern Portugal. Page 37.

shabby: not honorable or fair; unacceptable. Page 123.

shock rock: a designation for a combination of rock music with elements of theatrical shock value designed to push the current limits of decency, such as wearing bizarre makeup and costumes, smashing guitars, blowing up props, throwing things at the audience and other actions violating acceptable protocol for live performance. Page 24.

shot and shell: a reference to bullets or cannonballs (shot) and to metal containers filled with explosives that can be fired from a large gun over long distances (shell), used in warfare. Page 69.

shun: avoid, keep clear of. Page 123.

single-foot: a fast walking pace for a horse, in which each foot is lifted off the ground in turn. Page 39.

singularly: in a way that is concerned with one separate person or thing. Page 2.

sitar: a lute of India with a small, pear-shaped body and a long, broad, fretted (ridged) neck. Page 10.

slide(s): a part or mechanism that moves along a channel, groove or the like. Page 90.

snare (drum): a small double-headed drum having wires or strings stretched across the lower head. The top surface is struck using two wooden sticks and the vibration causes the wires on the underside to vibrate against the lower head, producing a rattling sound. Page 46.

Soul: a style of music that originated with black American gospel singing and is closely related to rhythm and blues. Soul (also *soul music*) is characterized by a pronounced beat and strong emotional quality. Page 23.

spiritual(s): a religious song, especially one arising from African-American culture. Page 67.

square dance: a lively dance with various steps and figures in which the couples are grouped in a given form, as a square. Page 44.

staid: settled, composed or unemotional in character. Page 37.

standard fare: literally, the usual type of food served or eaten. Used figuratively to refer to something else consumed or used. Page 33.

standard(s): a musical piece of sufficiently enduring popularity to be made part of a permanent repertoire, especially a popular song. Page 33.

stern-willed: a firm, strict or uncompromising attitude or manner. Page 123.

Stradivarius: a violin or other stringed instrument made by Antonio Stradivari (1644–1737) or his family. Stradivari established himself as the greatest violin maker in history. Page 112.

strain(s): a passage of music; tune. Page 7.

strife: strong disagreement or fighting; conflict. Page 69.

swing: a style of jazz or dance music with an easy-flowing but vigorous rhythm. Page 9.

synth: abbreviation for *synthesizer*. See **synthesizer.** Page 95.

synthesizer: any of various electronic consoles or modules, usually computerized, used to produce sounds unobtainable from ordinary musical instruments or to imitate instruments and voices. Page 2.

T

Tacoma: a seaport on the west coast of the United States, in the state of Washington. Page 2.

take, rough: a version of something, such as an instance of performing a musical piece, that is not yet perfect and polished. Page 36.

tangentially: in a way that has only slight relevance to some other topic or subject. Page 52.

tantamount: the same as or equivalent to a particular thing in effect, outcome or value. Page 112.

tap: open up, reach into, etc., for the purpose of using something; begin to use. Page 1.

tapestry: a piece of strong cloth decorated with pictures that are painted, embroidered or woven in colors, used for a wall hanging. Page 106.

Tenerife: the largest island of the Canary Islands, off the northwest coast of Africa. Page 38.

tentacles: figuratively, something that gradually or unnoticeably works its way into and around things and takes hold of them firmly or has a definite presence or effect. From the literal meaning, which is a long, flexible organ around the mouth or head of some animals, used for holding, grasping or moving. Page 123.

territory: an organized division of a country not having the full rights of a state. Used in reference to Alaska, which was a territory of the United States until it became a state in 1959. Page 13.

testament (to): something that shows that another thing exists or is true; evidence; proof. Page 65.

thirteen-note octave: in music, an *octave* is the span between any note and a note eight steps higher (from *octo,* eight). These eight steps are often referred to as *do, re, mi, fa, sol, la, ti, do.* The octave can also be broken down into smaller steps, so that thirteen such steps are heard from the lower note to the higher note. Page 62.

thumb piano: a hand-held African musical instrument consisting of a board with a row of tuned metal or wooden strips that vibrate when plucked by the thumb. Page 27.

Tibbett, Lawrence: (1896–1960) American baritone renowned for his success in both opera and motion pictures. Besides performing leading roles for twenty-seven seasons with the Metropolitan Opera in New York City, Tibbett was a popular figure in films and on radio. Page 16.

timple: a traditional Spanish stringed instrument of the Canary Islands. Page 12.

toboggan slide: a steep, rapid descent, such as the incline of snow and ice on which to slide in a *toboggan,* a long, narrow sled of thin boards turned up in front; from the Native North American name for this sled. Page 82.

Tone Scale (Emotional): a scale that shows the successive emotional tones a person can experience. By *tone* is meant the momentary or continuing emotional state of a person. Emotions such as fear, anger, grief, enthusiasm and others which people experience are shown on this graduated scale. A Tone Scale tells you how people behave. If people are at a certain level on the Tone Scale, then they behave in a certain way and you can predict how they will behave. Page 36.

track: a path in a recording that consists of one instrument, voice or the like. Many separate paths (tracks) can be combined together to create a final version, for example, of a piece of recorded music or a film. Page 51.

track, on the: in all past times. *Track* (also *time track*) means the timespan on which lies the consecutive record of events from the beginning (of something) to the present. (From *time track* of an individual, the timespan on which lies the consecutive record of events throughout a person's existence.) Page 82.

trade show: an event for dealers or the public of products by various manufacturers in a particular industry, usually held in a large exhibition hall, convention facility or the like. Page 60.

trailing: going off into something else, here used to describe the last few weeks or days of summer, the period before autumn begins. Page 44.

Treasure Island: a 1950 film adaptation of the 1883 novel by Scottish writer Robert Louis Stevenson (1850–1894), about a boy's voyage to Treasure Island to find buried treasure before pirates can reach it. Page 17.

treble: the higher audio frequencies. Treble sounds include cymbals, tinkling of bells, the higher notes of a trumpet, etc. Page 13.

trot: a way in which a horse moves that is faster than walking, in which a front leg and the opposite back leg are lifted together. Page 39.

troupe: a group of musicians, singers or other performers, especially one that travels from place to place. Page 31.

turn-of-the-century: of or having to do with the beginning or the end of the century (period of one hundred years) under consideration, here referring to the end of the 1800s and the beginning of the 1900s. Page 10.

𝒰

ubiquitous: present, appearing or to be found everywhere. Page 21.

ukulele: (shortened form *uke*) a small stringed instrument related to the guitar. It has four strings that are strummed with one hand while the player presses the strings on the neck. The ukulele was developed from a small guitar brought to Hawaii by the Portuguese in the late 1800s. Page 2.

ultraslick: characterized by extremely good execution and polished sophistication. Page 76.

unbridled: not controlled or restrained. Page 38.

underpinning: that which forms the basis or foundation of something. Literally, a system of supports beneath a wall or the like. Page 121.

under-rhythm: another name for *counter-rhythm. See also* **counter-rhythm.** Page 76.

unpositive: not firm or certain; imprecise. Page 11.

upbeats: *beat* refers to a regular emphasis or pulse of sound. For example, a common beat for rock music consists of a repeating pattern of four beats at regular intervals. In this instance, each of these four beats is a downbeat. If counted out loud, one would hear "ONE and TWO and THREE and FOUR," the four numbers being the *downbeats,* or *strong* beats. The "and" between each number would be an *upbeat,* or *weak* beat. Page 22.

up to anything, isn't really: not capable of undertaking or producing anything. Page 54.

Vallee, Rudy: (1901–1986) stage name of Hubert Prior Vallee, who, as a professional musician, formed his own dance band and became one of the most popular singers of the 1920s. He later moved into other areas of entertainment and became a comedian and actor in Hollywood, appearing in a number of films. Page 83.

venue(s): the place where something happens, especially an event such as a concert. Page 38.

vocal inflection: change or variation of pitch (high and low) or loudness of the voice. Page 24.

voodoo drums: drums, played in groups of three varying sizes, used in voodoo ceremonies. *Voodoo* is a body of beliefs and practices originally from Africa that includes magic and the supposed exercise of supernatural powers through the aid of spirits. Page 17.

VU meter: a *volume unit meter*. A meter used with sound-reproducing or recording equipment that indicates average sound levels. Page 84.

weather vane: figuratively, something that indicates the direction of a tendency or trend, from the literal meaning of *weather vane,* a device, usually mounted on a roof, that turns to point in the direction that the wind is blowing. Page 52.

West Indies: a large group of islands between North America and South America in the North Atlantic. Page 65.

West Virginia: a mountainous state in the east central United States, about 100 miles (160 kilometers) west of Washington, DC. West Virginia lies within the *Appalachians,* a mountain system of eastern North America, nearly parallel with the Atlantic coast and extending from the province of Quebec in Canada to northern Alabama, in the southern area of the United States. Page 81.

WOL: the group of letters (termed *call letters*) that identify a radio transmitting station, in this case a radio station located in Washington, DC. Radio WOL began operating in the late 1920s, making it one of the oldest radio stations in Washington, DC. Page 10.

Wurlitzer: a type of large electronic organ made by the Rudolph Wurlitzer Company. Page 21.

Y

yearn: have a deep longing or desire (for something). Page 69.

Z

zither, Chinese: also called *qin,* an ancient Chinese musical instrument. The qin consists of a flat wooden soundbox across which are seven strings that are plucked by the performer. Page 10.

INDEX

Palm Springs, California, photograph, 47

performer, 1

photographer, 1

poet, 1

real time and mix line mixer, 110

recordist, 36, 110

screenwriter, 1

I

India

sitar, 10

instructor

L. Ron Hubbard, 36

instrumentation

arranging and, 67

instruments, 7, 26–27

Aborigine rhythm sticks, 27

African shaker instruments, 26

African split wooden drums (Gatos), 26

African square drum, 27

African thumb pianos, 27

African wind instrument, 26

Appalachian cherry-wood dulcimer, 26

Australian didgeridoo, 26

bamboo flute, 27

banjo, 2, 10

self-taught, 7

banjo, five-string (1880), 27

banjo, five-string (turn-of-the-century), 27

billibutugun, 2, 9

bongos, 26

castanets acquired in Spain (1953), 27

congas, 23

electronic synthesizer, 2

five-string timple, 12

Gaelic harp, 26

gamelan gongs, 10

guitar, 13

guitar, classical, six-string, 27

guitar, tiple, 13

harmonicas, 2

Hohner, 27

self-taught, 7

Himalayan stringed instrument, 26

how to separate out, 50

India

sitar, 10

koto

Japan, 10

L. Ron Hubbard's collection, 96

maracas, 26, 27

Martin ten-string "Tiple," 13, 26

Native African drums, 26

organs, 88–94

"Pineapple" Uke, 26

proportionate sound and, 49

saxophone, 10

self-taught, 7

sound and separation of, 49

spin drums, 27

Syrian drum, 26

tenor guitar (four-string), 26

timple, 12, 26

tribal war drums

Mongolia, 10

trombone, English-crafted, 27

ukulele, 2, 12

Venezuelan baritone cuatro, 26

Wurlitzer, 21, 89

zither

China, 10

THE
L. RON HUBBARD
SERIES

"To really know life," L. Ron Hubbard wrote, "you've got to be part of life. You must get down and look, you must get into the nooks and crannies of existence. You have to rub elbows with all kinds and types of men before you can finally establish what he is."

Through his long and extraordinary journey to the founding of Dianetics and Scientology, Ron did just that. From his adventurous youth in a rough and tumble American West to his far-flung trek across a still mysterious Asia; from his two-decade search for the very essence of life to the triumph of Dianetics and Scientology—such are the stories recounted in the L. Ron Hubbard Biographical Publications.

Drawn from his own archival collection, this is Ron's life as he himself saw it. With each volume of the series focusing upon a separate field of endeavor, here are the compelling facts, figures, anecdotes and photographs from a life like no other.

Indeed, here is the life of a man who lived at least twenty lives in the space of one.

FOR FURTHER INFORMATION VISIT
www.lronhubbard.org

To order copies of *The L. Ron Hubbard Series*
or L. Ron Hubbard's Dianetics and
Scientology books and lectures, contact:

US and International

Bridge Publications, Inc.
5600 E. Olympic Blvd.
Commerce, California 90022 USA
www.bridgepub.com
Tel: (323) 888-6200
Toll-free: 1-800-722-1733

United Kingdom and Europe

New Era Publications
International ApS
Smedeland 20
2600 Glostrup, Denmark
www.newerapublications.com
Tel: (45) 33 73 66 66
Toll-free: 00-800-808-8-8008